Gemma McFarlane

GLUTEN-, NUT-, EGG- & DAIRY-FREE
Celebration Cakes

42 simple and delicious recipes for bakers and cake decorators

First published in December 2012
by B. Dutton Publishing Limited,
The Grange, Hones Business Park,
Farnham, Surrey, GU9 8BB.

Copyright: Gemma McFarlane 2012
ISBN-13: 978-1-905113-41-5

Publisher: Beverley Dutton

Group Editor: Jenny Stewart

Art Director/Designer: Sarah Ryan

Contributing Editor: Jo Hill

Editor: Jenny Royle

Designer: Zena Deakin

Graphic Designer: Louise Pepé

Copy Editor: Amy Norman

Editorial Assistants: Frankie New, Adele Duthie

Photography: Alister Thorpe, Giles Jenkyn

Printed in Slovenia

I'd like to thank and dedicate this book to Simon, my amazing, patient, loving husband who for years has tasted recipes, washed up for me at two in the morning, made my fabulous website and supported me tirelessly through work and life.

Acknowledgements

I would like to thank Beverley Dutton and everyone at Squires Kitchen who has helped to make this book what it is: Jenny Stewart, Frankie New and Jo Hill for making sense of my words; Helen Wingfield for her technical advice; Sarah Ryan for making this book look truly amazing; and Alister Thorpe and Giles Jenkyn for their brilliant photography.

Important Information

The Author and Publisher have made every effort to ensure that the information given in this book is correct at the time of writing and, if followed carefully, will not cause harm or injury or pose any danger. However, any information given is not a substitute for medical advice. Readers should be aware of any legislation that may have been introduced since this book was published.

Manufacturers of the foods recommended in this book may change the ingredients at any time and without notice. Consumers and cake makers who are concerned about food allergies must be aware of this risk and should always check the label on food products.

Please note that some inedible items, such as flower stamens and cake dowels, have been used in the projects in this book. All such inedible items must be removed before the cake is eaten. Similarly, any non food-grade equipment and substances, such as non-toxic glue, must not come into contact with any cake or cake covering that is to be eaten.

Neither the Author nor the Publisher can be held responsible for errors or omissions and cannot accept liability for injury, damage or loss to persons or property, however it may arise, as a result of acting upon guidelines and information printed in this book.

Introduction

Whether it's a wedding or christening, a children's party or Christmas gathering, the celebration cake is the centrepiece of any occasion. Yet I am constantly amazed by the number of people with special diets who haven't enjoyed a birthday cake for years – or ever!

Shop-bought cakes, if available, can be bland and boring and many cake makers are reluctant to take orders for special diets. They may be nervous about catering for certain requirements or unsure about using alternative ingredients; either way, it means many people are missing out on the simple pleasure of a well-made cake.

In this book, I have set out to dispel the myths about baking for special diets and show you how to make show-stopping celebration cakes that are every bit as delicious as traditional versions.

There are over 30 recipes and plenty of advice on a whole range of special diets including dairy free, egg free, wheat free, gluten free and vegan with suggestions for making all of them nut free; information about how to avoid cross-contamination; and hints and tips for decorating fabulous cakes as well as 13 celebration cake projects to cater for all occasions. So if you're a professional cake maker who's fed up with turning down orders, or you want to make beautiful creations for friends and family in your own kitchen, this book will show you that catering for special diets really is a piece of cake!

Gemma

Contents

ALL YOU NEED TO KNOW BEFORE MAKING SPECIAL-DIET CAKES

About Me

I became interested in cakes and cooking from an early age, watching my gran who was always in the kitchen.

I trained and worked as a chef for 12 years, starting as a commis chef in a private hospital. My next job was as head cook in a home for children and young adults with severe learning difficulties. During that time I catered for many people with special diets: gluten free, lactose free, egg free, sodium free and other allergies. I would adapt dishes to suit individual needs so they could have the same meal as everyone else. As a result, I became determined to offer the same choices to everyone so began researching and experimenting with different ingredients.

This sparked my interest in cooking for special diets. While working as a pastry chef I began experimenting with ingredients and produced a range of vegan, gluten-free and lactose-free cakes.

I also enjoyed making celebration cakes so I enrolled in evening classes and completed a City and Guilds in Sugarcraft. In 2006 I started my own business, Iced Gem Cakes, making celebration cakes and supplying local cafés with special-diet cakes. I was especially proud to be able to offer a coeliac bride a wedding cake or a child with a food allergy a birthday cake they could eat themselves. I took requests for special-diet celebration cakes from people all over the country who couldn't find anyone closer to make their cake. That is why I decided to write this book, so that hopefully more cake decorators will make these cakes for their customers and home bakers can have a go themselves.

All You Need to Know

Before Making Special-diet Cakes

I am a chef, and although I have been catering for special diets for many years, I am not a medical professional. Therefore, I have taken the following information about allergies and intolerances from the Food Standards Agency. Please check the FSA website for the latest advice on food allergies (see page 168).

If you think you have a food allergy or intolerance, you should always speak to a healthcare professional before cutting foods out of your diet. For more information about food allergies and intolerances, visit the Food Standards Agency website or the NHS website (see page 168).

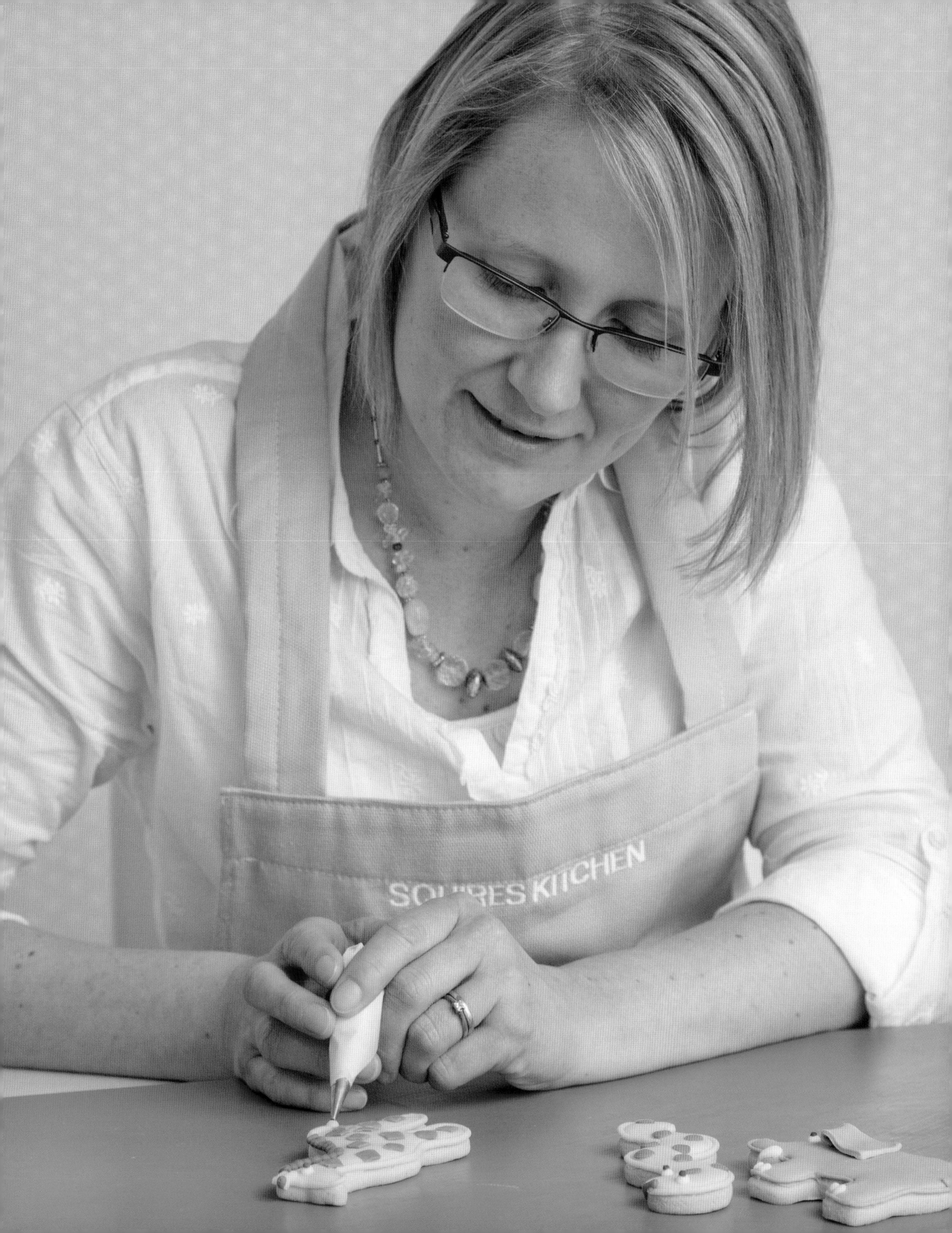
SQUIRES KITCHEN

About Food Allergies

A food allergy is caused when the immune system thinks certain foods are harmful to the body. An allergic reaction can occur as soon as a food is eaten or up to a few hours later. There is no cure. An allergy can only be managed by completely cutting specific foods out of a person's diet and by ensuring that the food they do eat has not come into contact with the allergen.

Anti-allergy medication can be used to relieve allergy symptoms. For mild reactions, antihistamines can be used, but for a severe anaphylactic reaction, which can be life-threatening, an injection of adrenaline is required. People with severe allergies should always carry an auto-injector of adrenaline with them. Visit the NHS website[1] for more information.

There are 14 known allergens (see pages 14 to 15) but the most common foods to cause allergies are:

Milk

Eggs

Peanuts

Tree nuts (including walnuts and brazil nuts)

Fish

Shellfish (including crab and prawns)

Some types of fruit and vegetables (including apples, pears, potatoes and carrots)

By law, all of the 14 listed allergens have to be highlighted on the label if contained in a food product, including unpackaged foods.

Common symptoms of a food allergy are:

Dry, itchy throat and tongue

Itchy skin and rash

Nausea and feeling bloated

Diarrhoea and/or vomiting

Wheezing and shortness of breath

Swelling of lips and throat

Coughing

Runny or blocked nose

Sore, red and itchy eyes

[1]www.nhs.uk/conditions/food-allergy/

About Food Intolerance

A food intolerance is different from a food allergy and can be caused by the body's inability to digest certain foods. It is not usually life-threatening, but can make a person very ill or adversely affect their long-term health.

People with food intolerances can usually consume small amounts of the food they are intolerant to without getting ill, although this does vary from person to person. The most common symptoms can include diarrhoea, weight loss, bloating and anaemia.

Diagnosing a food intolerance other than coeliac disease and lactose intolerance is difficult. One method is to eliminate the specific food from your diet, but you should always speak to your doctor before doing this.

Coeliac disease

It is estimated that one in 100 people in the UK has coeliac disease[2]. Coeliac disease is an autoimmune condition which means that the body has a reaction to a trigger – in this case, gluten – causing the body to attack itself.

For coeliacs, eating even the tiniest amount of gluten causes the lining of the small intestine to become damaged, preventing the normal absorption of nutrients. Other parts of the body may also be affected. However, the good news is that cutting out foods containing gluten will gradually help the stomach lining to return to normal.

Gluten is found naturally in wheat, barley and rye, and is often found in oats when cross-contamination occurs during the milling process. 'Pure' oats are available, but whilst these are free from contamination, some coeliacs may still suffer an adverse reaction because oats contain a similar protein to gluten.

The standard set for the whole of the EU is a maximum level of 20 parts per million (ppm) of gluten in order for foods to be labelled as 'gluten-free' and 100ppm of gluten for foods labelled as 'very low gluten' (restricted to foods processed to remove gluten). The new regulations align EU law with the Codex for international food standards. If you live outside Europe, please check the limit set for your country.

Symptoms of coeliac disease include diarrhoea, anaemia, weight loss, fatigue, bloating and sickness. If you

[2]www.coeliac.org.uk/coeliac-disease/myths-about-coeliac-disease

have these symptoms your doctor can refer you for a blood test to diagnose a gluten intolerance[3].

Wheat intolerance

According to the Food Standards Agency, wheat intolerance – which is not the same as gluten intolerance – is thought to be one of the more common food intolerances. Diagnosing a food intolerance other than coeliac disease and lactose intolerance is difficult, but symptoms can include bloating, headaches and joint pain. People suffering from these symptoms may choose to cut wheat from their diet for a period of time and see if this alleviates the symptoms. You should always speak to your doctor before doing this. For more information, visit the website below[4].

Lactose intolerance

Lactose is a sugar found in the milk of all animals and therefore contained in butter, cream, yoghurt and other milk products. This intolerance is caused by a lack of the enzyme required to digest lactose – although some sufferers are able to cope with small amounts. Symptoms usually include a bloated and painful stomach, weight loss and diarrhoea. For more information, visit the website below[5].

Egg intolerance

Egg allergy or intolerance is also common, especially in young children, although many grow out of it by the age of five or six. Symptoms include itchiness, rash, stomach cramps, nausea and breathing problems[6].

Cooking with eggs can also bring on symptoms. When checking packaging, be aware that egg may also be labelled as albumen (see page 20).

[3]www.nhs.uk/livewell/allergies/pages/foodallergy.aspx [4]www.allergyuk.org/fs_wheat.aspx
[5]www.nhs.uk/conditions/Lactose-intolerance/Pages/Introduction.aspx [6]www.nhs.uk/conditions/food-allergy/Pages/Intro1.aspx

Other Special Diets

Vegan

Vegans do not eat any foods of animal origin. This includes meat, fish, dairy foods, and also honey. For more information, visit www.vegansociety.com.

Diabetes

Diabetes develops when the body can't process glucose properly. As a result, diabetics can have abnormally high levels of glucose in their blood if the condition isn't controlled.

People with diabetes should try to maintain a healthy weight and eat a diet that is:

Low in fat (particularly saturated fat);

Low in sugar;

Low in salt;

High in fruit and vegetables (at least five portions a day);

High in starchy carbohydrate foods such as bread, chapatti, rice, pasta and yams, preferably wholegrain varieties. These should form the base of meals.

There are no foods that people with diabetes should avoid completely – cakes and biscuits can be enjoyed sparingly as part of a balanced diet. Whilst there is no need to cut out all sugar, diabetics – like everyone – should try to eat only small amounts of foods that are high in sugar and/or fat. For more information, visit www.diabetes.org.uk.

Halal

Halal is the description of food and drink allowed by Muslims under Islamic dietary laws. Alcohol is forbidden, and in cake making this would include alcohol in vanilla extract or other flavourings and some food colourings. Powder or dust food colours can be diluted for painting with rose water instead of alcohol.

For more information visit www.halalfoodauthority.co.uk.

Kosher

Jewish dietary laws state that meat and dairy products may not be made or consumed together. If a Kosher food is cooked in the same oven as a non-Kosher food, then it becomes non-Kosher.

Utensils and equipment used for non-Kosher food preparation cannot be used for cooking Kosher food. However, disposable equipment can be used. Ovens, stove tops, fridges, microwaves and dishwashers need to be scrupulously cleaned in a certain way before use.

For more information about cooking for a Kosher diet in a non-Kosher kitchen, visit www.hanefesh.com/edu/Kosher_Kitchen.htm.

More information about Kosher diets can be found at www.kosherfood.about.com.

Food Allergy Labelling

Under European Union regulations introduced in October 2011, professional cake makers who sell directly to the final consumer or to local retail establishments directly supplying the final consumer must label their cakes with relevant allergen information in the same way as they would label packaged products. Make sure that all information is accurate and cannot be seen as misleading. If you live outside the EU, make sure you check the relevant labelling legislation for your country.

Allergens and where they are commonly found

You must provide information if your product contains any of the following allergens or ingredients derived from the following allergens:

Name of Allergen	Commonly Found In
Peanuts and products thereof	Sauces, cakes, desserts, groundnut oil, peanut flour.
Nuts and products thereof, namely: almonds, hazelnuts, walnuts, cashews, pecan nuts, brazil nuts, pistachio nuts and macadamia nuts, except for nuts used for making alcoholic distillates including ethyl alcohol of agricultural origin.	Sauces, desserts, crackers, bread, ice cream, marzipan, ground almonds, nut oils.
Soybeans and products thereof, except: (a) fully refined soybean oil and fat (1); (b) natural mixed tocopherols (E306), natural D-alpha tocopherol, natural D-alpha tocopherol acetate, and natural D-alpha tocopherol succinate from soybean sources; (c) vegetable oils derived phytosterols and phytosterol esters from soybean sources; (d) plant stanol ester produced from vegetable oil sterols from soybean sources.	Tofu or beancurd, soya flour and textured soya protein, some ice creams, yoghurts, sauces, desserts, meat products, vegetarian products, ready-made meals, margarine, lecithin.
Mustard and products thereof, including liquid mustard, mustard powder and mustard seeds.	Salad dressings, marinades, soups, sauces, curries, meat products.
Lupin and products thereof	Lupin seeds and flour found in some types of bread and pastries.
Eggs and products thereof	Cakes, mousses, sauces, pasta, quiche, some meat products, mayonnaise, foods brushed with egg.

Name of Allergen	Commonly Found In
Fish and products thereof, except: a) fish gelatine used as a carrier for vitamin or carotenoid preparations; b) fish gelatine or isinglass used as fining agent in beer and wine.	Some salad dressings, pizzas, relishes, fish sauce and some soy and Worcestershire sauces.
Crustaceans and products thereof	Shrimps, prawns, scampi, crab, shrimp paste, crayfish, lobster.
Cereals containing gluten, namely: wheat, rye, barley, oats, spelt, Kamut, or their hybridised strains, and products thereof, except: a) wheat-based glucose syrups including dextrose; b) wheat-based maltodextrins; c) glucose syrup based on barley; d) cereals used for making alcohol distillates including ethyl alcohol of agricultural origin.	Cereals such as wheat, rye and barley and foods containing flour, such as bread, pasta, cakes, pastry, meat products, sauces, soups, batter, stock cubes, breadcrumbs, food dusted with flour. Most oats are also contaminated with gluten-containing cereals in the milling process.
Sesame seeds and products thereof	Bread, breadsticks, tahini, hummus, sesame oil.
Celery and products thereof, including celery stalks, leaves and seeds and celeriac.	Salads, soups, celery salt, some meat products.
Sulphur dioxide and sulphites at concentrations of more than 10mg/kg or 10mg/litre in terms of the total SO2 which are to be calculated for products as proposed ready for consumption or as reconstituted according to the instructions of the manufacturers.	Meat products, fruit juice drinks, dried fruit and vegetables, wine and beer.
Milk and products thereof, including cream, butter, cheese, yogurt, except: a) whey used for making alcoholic distillates including ethyl alcohol of agricultural origin; b) lactitol.	Many ready-made foods.
Molluscs and products thereof	Abalone, clams, mussels, octopus, oysters, squid and scallops.

If you are still using one or more of six food colourings that are being voluntarily phased out, you must include a warning on products. In addition to the standard required information, labels must also have a warning using the following wording: '[the name or E number of the colour(s)] may have an adverse effect on activity and attention in children.' This must be declared all food that contains the colours, even non pre-packed food.

The colours are:

Sunset yellow (E110)

Quinoline yellow (E104)

Carmoisine (E122)

Allura red (E129)

Tartrazine (E102)

Ponceau 4R (E124)

Example form

Company name:

Contact: .... Phone number: .... Website: ....

Cake flavour:

Please note this cake contains:

[any of the allergens] or [any of the six listed food colourings. Exxx: May have an adverse effect on activity and attention in children].

Additional information:

This cake has been made suitable for a [gluten-free/nut-free/vegan, etc] diet.

Special instructions:

Please store at room temperature/in a cool room/in a fridge.

Inedible decorations or dowels must be removed before serving the cake.

This cake has been made without [gluten-containing] ingredients at the request of [name]..

To prevent cross contamination please use a clean knife for cutting and serve on a labelled tray separate from any other cake.

Personally, I feel it is always good practice to provide dietary information about my cakes, particularly those for special diets. When I deliver a celebration cake to a venue, I always leave a compliment slip detailing the cake flavour, whether the cake contains any of the main allergens (as per the labelling regulations, see pages 14 to 15), information about any dowels or inedible decorations and my contact details.

If the cake is suitable for a special diet I will also highlight this and leave any special instructions for serving.

From 1st January 2012, caterers can no longer label food as gluten free unless the food has been tested for the gluten levels. Caterers will be able to state 'No gluten-containing ingredients' and can provide additional information to back this up. If you do this, it is advisable to check with your local Trading Standards that you are doing this correctly (see page 168). On a larger scale, food manufacturers are generally becoming more aware of food allergies and intolerances. Many are changing ingredients so that they are suitable for more people or making alternative products for people with allergies or intolerances.

Since November 2005, food labelling has increasingly improved for those with a food intolerance or allergy, making shopping a lot easier, and this will only improve further following the November 2011 Information for Consumers Regulation[7].

Anyone making and selling pre-packed cakes or bakery products must label their products with the following information:

(a) The name of the food;

(b) The list of ingredients;

(c) Any of the 14 listed allergens or products thereof;

(d) The quantity of certain ingredients or categories of ingredients;

(e) The net quantity of the food;

(f) The 'use by' date;

(g) Any special storage conditions and/ or conditions of use;

(h) The name or business name and address of the food business operator;

(i) The country of origin;

(j) Instructions for use where it would be difficult to make appropriate use of the food in the absence of such instructions;

(k) With respect to beverages containing more than 1.2% by volume of alcohol, the actual alcoholic strength by volume;

(l) A nutrition declaration.

Allergy boxes or 'May contain' statements on packaging are voluntary. If the food contains any of the listed allergens, this must be labelled in the ingredient list using a different font so it stands out from the rest of the ingredients.

[7]http://tinyurl.com/7vhme3q

Preventing Cross-Contamination

It is essential that food providers give accurate information about what is in their products to protect their customers from becoming ill. Just a tiny amount of food may make a person with an allergy or food intolerance seriously ill, so the utmost care must be taken to avoid contamination. If you are making a cake for somebody with a severe allergy, discuss with them the allergens in your kitchen and the ingredients you will be using to make sure they are completely happy for you to make their cake.

Much of the following advice may seem obvious, but I always think it is reassuring to have, particularly for those who are not used to cooking for those on a special diet or are not confident cooks.

Ordering

Check the ingredients on all foods to be given to people with special diets. Refer to the label each time you buy a product as ingredients change all the time.

If you buy your ingredients from a wholesaler, ask them to provide you with the food specifications for all products. Keep a file of these and make a list of ingredients containing allergens.

Be aware of other names for allergens such as those included on the list on page 20.

If you are unsure about an ingredient contact the manufacturer: their details should be on the packaging.

Storage

Store ingredients in separate, lidded, washable containers labelled with the contents and use-by date.

Store foods containing allergens in separate cupboards to other ingredients.

Preparing food

Ensure all worktops and equipment are scrupulously clean before preparing food. Always wash your hands before preparing or handling food.

I recommend keeping a separate set of basic utensils for each special diet to protect against cross-contamination. These are:

- A sieve;
- A pastry rolling pin;
- A silicone brush (this can be cleaned easily and is more hygienic than a pastry brush);
- A chopping board for bread, pastry and cakes;
- A whisk;
- Oven gloves.

Not many kitchens are completely free of allergens, so care must be taken at all times to avoid cross-contamination. The following guidelines may seem strict, but they are essential when catering for special diets and soon become second nature:

• Use separate tubs of margarine and butter for special-diet cakes. Alternatively, ensure you always put a clean utensil into the tub.

• When spreading jam onto a cake, don't put the spreading knife into the jam jar as it will transfer crumbs into the jar. Instead, spoon the jam onto the sponge and use a separate palette knife for spreading.

• Use separate scoops for dry ingredients.

• Keep a large nylon piping bag just for dairy-free fillings.

• When weighing or sifting flours or nuts, be sure that there are no open tubs of other ingredients around you. Use a separate spoon to add cocoa powder to flour.

• Prepare, cook and store special-diet cakes separately to other cakes.

• Do not cook special-diet cakes and 'normal' cakes in the same oven together.

• If a multi-tiered cake contains a special-diet cake tier, prepare, fill and cover this layer away from the others and using clean utensils. Alternatively, prepare and fill one type of cake then clean all equipment and work surfaces before preparing the other. Make sure

each tier is placed on a cake board or cake card before it is stacked.

• If only one tier of a stacked cake is to be made suitable for a special diet, make sure this is the top tier and place it onto a cake board or card, as above. If you stack a 'normal' cake on top of a special-diet cake it could transfer allergens. If this doesn't provide enough portions you could make an extra cutting cake.

• Do not use the same knife to cut through a special-diet cake and a 'normal' cake.

• If you have any leftover buttercream, sugarpaste or marzipan, cover and label it with the type of cake you used it on and which allergens the cake contains.

• If you are not sure what sort of cake you used an open packet of sugarpaste, marzipan or buttercream for, do not use it for a special-diet cake.

• Remember that fortified egg white contains wheat. Always use fresh egg white or pure albumen for royal icing on wheat-free cakes. If you are unsure, check the ingredients.

• Always use a clean knife or new cocktail stick when adding colouring to food.

• Check the ingredients in flower paste and modelling paste (see list on page 157) to make sure they are suitable for decorating the cake. If you make your own, check the ingredients of the glucose syrup, egg white and white vegetable fat. Make sure the white fat hasn't been in contact with flour from pastry making.

• Use fresh brandy for brushing onto cakes. Never pour leftover brandy back into the bottle. (Remember that some diets don't allow alcohol, see page 13.)

• Check the ingredients on all sugarcraft ingredients before use.

• Clean sugarcraft cutters and tools after each use.

Serving

Inform your customer when they order their special-diet cake that you use ingredients containing allergens in your kitchen. If a customer asks a question about whether a food contains an allergen, make sure you are completely sure of your answer.

When giving a special-diet cake to the customer or especially if you are dropping off a cake at a venue, leave a note with the cake informing the customer of the flavour, dietary information and any allergens which the cake does or may contain (see the example form on page 16).

Leave any special instructions for serving, such as:

'To prevent cross-contamination please use a clean knife for cutting and serve separately from any other cake on a labelled tray.'

TOP TIP

Cakes made without gluten-containing ingredients or vegan cakes are crumblier than regular cakes so I suggest using a hot, clean knife with each cut for easier portioning.

Hidden Ingredients

Many ingredients in processed foods which are derived from cereals, dairy products and eggs may have different names. Nuts and peanuts must be listed clearly on food labels. The ingredients listed below are other names for the ingredient at the top. Always look for the allergy information on the label as this must be declared by law.

Gluten	Wheat	Dairy/Lactose	Egg	Nuts
Modified starch, unless it is labelled modified maize starch	Modified starch, unless it is labelled modified maize starch	Milk from all animals and milk products including cream, yoghurt, butter and cheese*	Albumin/albumen	**Peanuts:**
			Conalbumin	Peanut oil
Wheat flour	Wheat flour		Globulin	Ground nut (ground nut oil)
Wheat starch and modified wheat starch	Wheat starch and modified wheat starch	Whey*	Livetin	Arachis oil
			Lysozyme	Arachide
Wheat rusk	Wheat rusk	Whey powder*	Meringue	Beer nut
Wheat bran	Wheat bran	Whey protein*		Monkey nuts
Barley malt	Cereal binder, unless labelled as wheat free	Whey solids*	Ovalbumin	Mixed nuts
Barley flour		Casein	Ovoglobulin	
Oat bran	Rusk, unless labelled as wheat free	Calcium casein	Ovolactohydrolyze proteins	**Tree nuts:**
Rye flour		Caseinate	Ovomacroglobulin	Almond
Bran		Lactal bumin	Ovomucin, ovomucoid	Beechnut
Cereal binder, unless labelled as safe for a gluten-free diet		Milk powder	Ovotransferrin	Brazil nut
		Skimmed milk powder	Ovovitellin	Bush nut
Rusk, unless labelled as safe for a gluten-free diet.		Milk solids	Silico-albuminate	Butternut
		Non fat milk solids	Vitellin and vitellenin	Cashew
		Lactate		Chestnut
		Milk derivative		Coconut
				Filbert
				Ginko nut
				Hazelnut
				Hickory nut
				Lichee nut
				Macadamia nut
				Nangai nut
				Pecan
				Pine nut (pinyon nut)
				Pistachio
				Shea nut
				Walnut
				Artificial nuts
				Pure nut extracts

*Please note these products may also be unsuitable for vegetarians because they may contain rennet.

The Wheat-, Gluten- and Lactose-free Store Cupboard

If you are catering for somebody with an allergy or intolerance, it is vital you know what is in all of your ingredients. Go to the 'Sugarcraft Products Containing Glucose Syrup' section for more dietary information about popular brands of sugarcraft ingredients (see page 25).

Overleaf is my essential list of long-life ingredients that I use in many of my recipes for special diets. A list of stockists can be found on page 168.

If you are baking for a nut-free diet, you must ensure that any ingredients on the list that contain (or may contain) nuts are excluded from your kitchen completely.

Store cupboard essentials

INGREDIENT	Gluten Free?	Dairy Free?	Vegan?	Nut-free?
Specially-blended gluten-free flour: I use Doves Farm gluten-free plain flour, which is a blend of rice, potato, tapioca, maize and buckwheat flours. This is available in most supermarkets.	YES	YES	YES	Check label
Maize flour: known as cornflour in America, this is yellow and milled as fine as flour. Infinity Foods produce a good variety, labelled as cornflour.	YES	YES	YES	Check label
Cornflour: this is called cornstarch in America. Available in supermarkets, it is white in colour and can be used to thicken sauces.	YES	YES	YES	Check label
Gram flour (chickpea flour): available from whole food shops and supermarkets.	YES	YES	YES	Check label
Ground almonds: available in whole food shops and supermarkets.	YES	YES	YES	NO
Tapioca flour: available from whole food shops and Asian supermarkets.	YES	YES	YES	Check label
Xanthan gum: available from whole food shops and supermarkets. This is made by fermenting corn sugar. I only use this for bread recipes as I have found it is not necessary for cakes or pastries.	YES	YES	YES	Check label
Gluten-free baking powder: this is readily available in supermarkets. It works exactly the same as ordinary baking powder and can also be used when baking wheat products. I only keep gluten-free baking powder in my store cupboard so I don't get mixed up with that containing wheat.	YES	YES	YES	Check label
Bicarbonate of soda: available from supermarkets.	YES	YES	YES	Check label
White wine or cider vinegar: used as a raising agent in my vegan cakes.	YES	YES	YES	Check label
Coconut milk: milk made from the pulp of the coconut, available in supermarkets.	YES	YES	YES	Check label
Coconut cream: available from some supermarkets, whole food shops or Asian supermarkets.	YES	YES	YES	Check label
Creamed coconut: available from some supermarkets, whole food shops or Asian supermarkets.	YES	YES	YES	Check label
Sweetened or original soya milk: available from supermarkets, whole food shops and Asian supermarkets.	YES	YES	YES	Check label
Almond milk: available from supermarkets, whole food shops and Asian supermarkets.	YES	YES	YES	NO
Sunflower oil: available from supermarkets, whole food shops and Asian supermarkets.	YES	YES	YES	Check label

Store cupboard essentials

INGREDIENT	Gluten Free?	Dairy Free?	Vegan?	Nut-free?
Dairy-free margarine: supermarkets and other stores stock different brands of this. They do vary so it is worth trying different brands until you find one you like. I've carried out my own taste tests and at the moment my favourite is Vitalite® dairy-free fat spread.	Check label, mainly gluten free	YES	YES	Check label
Dairy- and gluten-free plain chocolate (55–60% cocoa solids): available from supermarkets, specialist chocolate shops, whole food shops and Asian supermarkets. I use chocolate with 55–60% cocoa solids in my recipes. Chocolate with a higher percentage of cocoa solid will make ganache and chocolate paste too firm to use in my particular recipes (see pages 82, 84 and 95).	YES	YES	YES	Check label
Dairy-free white and milk chocolate: this is becoming more widely available from supermarkets and can also be found in whole food stores and Asian supermarkets. Some brands of dairy-free white chocolate will not work in some recipes, for example in ganache, so make sure you trial any recipe first.	YES	YES	YES	Check label
Pure cocoa powder: check on the packaging whether this is gluten- and dairy-free. Hot chocolate powder usually contains wheat.	Check label	Check label	Check label	Check label
Gluten- and dairy-free chocolate chips: available from Plamil® in small tubs and in bulk quantities.	YES	YES	YES	Check label
White vegetable fat: available from supermarkets.	Check label	Check label	Check label	Check label
Glycerine: ensure this is suitable for vegans. Available from supermarkets, chemists and sugarcraft suppliers.	YES	YES	Check label	Check label
Gluten-free food flavourings and extracts: available from supermarkets, whole food shops and Asian supermarkets.	Check label	Check label	Check label	Check label
Gluten-free food colouring: available from supermarkets, cook shops and specialist sugarcraft suppliers (see page 168).	Check label	Check label	Check label	Check label
Raisins, sultanas, currants: mainly gluten-free but some brands (mainly wholesale brands) use flour to stop the fruit sticking together.	Check label	YES	YES	Check label
Dried dates: some brands contain oat flour.	Check label	YES	YES	Check label
Wheat-free glacé cherries: available from supermarkets, whole food shops and Asian supermarkets.	Check label	YES	YES	Check label
Wheat-free mixed peel: the packaging should state if it is wheat free. Available from supermarkets, whole food shops and Asian supermarkets.	Check label	YES	YES	Check label

Store cupboard essentials

INGREDIENT	Gluten Free?	Dairy Free?	Vegan?	Nut-free?
Pure egg white powder: available from supermarkets, whole food shops and Asian supermarkets. This is different to Meri-white or fortified egg white powder which contains wheat.	Check label	Check label	Vegetarian but not suitable for vegans	Check label
Gum tragacanth: available from sugarcraft suppliers (see page 168).	YES	YES	YES	Check label
Gum arabic: a natural gum taken from the Acacia tree which is used as an edible glue in sugarcraft.	YES	YES	YES	Check label
Jam: some brands may contain dairy products or modified starch. Homemade jams may have a little butter added to disperse any scum, so always check the ingredients with whoever made it.	Check label	Check label	Check label	Check label
Rose water: use this for sticking sugar decorations together or onto cakes. Available from sugarcraft suppliers (see page 168)	Check label	YES	YES	Check label
Food flavourings: ingredients vary according to the brand so always check the label.	Check label	Check label	Check label	Check label
Food colouring: some older food colourings may be made with modified wheat starch. Most modern brands are safe for a wheat- and gluten-free diet.	Check label	Check label	Check label	Check label
Dust food colours: some powder colours contain lactose, so it's a good idea to label the lids of these products as a reminder. For more detailed dietary information, see page 159.	Check label	Check label	Check label	Check label
Ready-made cake decorations	Check label	Check label	Check label	Check label
Photo sheets and edible inks: most brands are safe for wheat-, gluten-, dairy- and egg-free diets. Always check with the supplier if using on cakes for special diets.	Check with supplier	Check with supplier	Check with supplier	Check label
Dr Oetker Vege Gel: this is a vegetarian gelatine substitute.	YES	YES	YES	Check label
Brandy suitable for vegans: Courvoisier cognac, Martell cognac or Co-operative Napolean Brandy.	YES	YES	YES	Check label
Dark rum suitable for vegans: Captain Morgan, Lamb's® Navy Rum, Co-operative Dark Rum.	YES	YES	YES	Check label
Vodka suitable for vegans (used for cake decoration): ABSOLUT VODKA®, Smirnoff®, Red Square, Co-operative Imperial Vodka.	YES	YES	YES	Check label

If you are buying ingredients through a catering wholesaler, ask for the ingredient specifications to be sure they are safe for people with special dietary requirements. Most wholesale ingredients such as glacé cherries, mixed peel or fondant contain glucose syrup derived from wheat (see further details opposite). Some brands of dried fruit may use flour (containing gluten) to stop them sticking together so always check the label.

Sugarcraft Products and their Allergens

Making celebration cakes for special diets can be a daunting prospect, and the dazzling range of icings and sugarcraft ingredients available in the UK can add to the confusion. To make things easier, I have compiled a simple, one-stop guide to food allergens found in the most commonly available sugarcraft products, starting on page 156.

It is worth noting the difference between a product that has been declared allergen-free (e.g. gluten free or nut free) and one that does not include any allergens in the ingredient list, but may contain traces of allergens. In order for a manufacturer to declare that a product is 'allergen-free' it must be tested and certified as such (see also page 17). Many products don't contain any ingredients that have allergens in them, but are not tested regularly or aren't from a 'free-from' factory, and therefore cannot be guaranteed 'allergen free'. If you are making special-diet cakes, you must ensure that all the ingredients you use do not contain allergens or traces of allergens, and that there is no risk from cross-contamination (see pages 18 to 19).

Product ingredients and their derivatives can change from batch to batch, so always check the label. The main variation I find is that the source of the glucose can change in every batch so it is wise to contact the manufacturer if you have particular concerns about wheat intolerance.

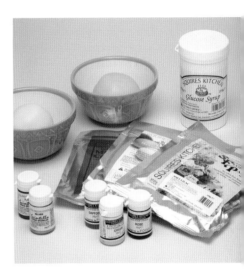

Sugarcraft products containing glucose syrup

There are hidden ingredients in all sorts of cake decorating products, some of which may come as a surprise (see pages 156 to 162). The biggest offender is glucose syrup, found in most sugarcraft products. Glucose can be made from any kind of starch and is used in sugary foods to soften texture and prevent the crystallisation of sugars.

In most of the world, glucose syrup comes from corn and is referred to as corn syrup rather than glucose syrup. In Europe, although it is made from corn, including wheat, glucose syrup is gluten-free due to the production methods used, in which the grain is highly processed.

Despite this, everyone has a different level of tolerance, and some people with a wheat and/or gluten intolerance say that it does affect them. So, for this reason, if I have a customer who can't eat wheat, I will also ask them if they are affected by glucose syrup or maltodextrin.

Manufacturers do not have to state what the glucose syrup in their products is derived from, so you will have to contact them to get this information. If you buy ingredients from a catering wholesaler, there is a good chance the glucose in the product will be made from wheat; this includes glacé cherries and mixed peel. Some wholesale brands of dried fruits such as raisins, sultanas and currants also contain flour to stop the fruit sticking together, although most use vegetable oil. Some dried figs are coated in oat flour.

As catering wholesalers do not have to declare where their glucose syrup derives from on their labels, to be absolutely sure about what is contained in a product, ask your supplier for the food specification list. This should contain a full ingredient list and information about their derivatives, the shelf life, ingredient origin and packaging information. Be aware, though, that ingredients and their derivatives change with every batch, so contact the supplier regularly for updated ingredient information if you are avoiding wheat derivatives as all allergens will always be labelled on the product. (Coeliacs need not regularly ask as they can eat glucose.)

You can request a product specification list with every batch of a product you purchase if needed.

Sugarcraft Tools

All of the sugarcraft tools and equipment used to decorate the cakes in this book are available from sugarcraft suppliers (see page 168). Specific sizes, quantities and colours are listed with each project, so you can make sure you have everything to hand before you start. The same risks of cross-contamination apply as with other tools and utensils, see page 18.

1 Ball tool or bone tool: a plastic tool with a different sized ball at each end, or with ends which look similar to a bone. Both are used to thin or frill petals and leaves made in sugar.

2 Cake smoother: a rectangular piece of smooth plastic with a handle on the back for smoothing sugarpaste or marzipan on a cake.

3 Cookie cutters: a set of cookie cutters suitable for children's biscuits. Choose a set that includes Christmas, Halloween and Easter cutters.

4 Craft knife: ideal for cutting out templates and small pieces of modelling paste.

5 Cutting wheel: used for cutting small shapes and strips from sugarpaste and modelling pastes.

6 Floral tape: to cover the wires of sugar flowers and to tape together floral arrangements.

7 Floral wires: available in a range of colours and gauges. The gauge refers to the thickness: 20-gauge being thick and 32-gauge being very fine. These are used to make sugar flowers and cake ornaments. Wires should only be used in decorations that won't be eaten and should never be inserted directly into a cake: always use a posy pick filled with paste (available from sugarcraft suppliers).

8 Flower nail: used for piping flowers onto as it can be turned easily with one hand while you pipe with the other.

9 Foam pad: a firm, food-grade pad that is used for thinning petals and leaves. Place them onto the pad and press onto the edges of the paste with a ball tool.

10 Great Impressions Petal and Leaf Veiners (SK): made from silicone rubber approved for food contact, veiners are used to emboss flower paste with realistic-looking veins and patterns. For the projects in this book I have used peony petal, rose leaf and poinsettia leaf veiners.

11 Hammerhead stamens: ready-made stamens used in flower making.

12 Large nylon piping bag: it is worth investing money in a good quality, nylon piping bag and Savoy nozzles. I regularly use these to make profiteroles and to ice cupcakes.

13 Multi-ribbon cutter (FMM): this tool has two cutting wheels with spacers in between which can be adapted to cut long strips of sugarpaste in varying widths.

14 Paintbrushes (SK): it is useful to have a range of sizes starting from 0 for fine painting to a flat no. 10 for dusting. Use good quality brushes with manmade bristles rather than sable (vital for vegan cakes) and keep only for sugarcraft use.

15 Piping nozzles (PME): I use metal nozzles to pipe detail onto cakes, cupcakes and cookies. The numbers required are given at the beginning of each project.

16 Stay fresh flexi-mat: a thick, clear plastic mat to place on top of rolled-out pastes to stop them drying out.

17 Stitching tool: used to mark a stitching pattern onto sugarpaste models.

18 Petal and leaf cutters: always useful for making flowers, I have used poinsettia (FMM), large rose leaf (OP) and small, medium and large rose petal cutters (TT) for the projects featured in this book.

19 Non-stick board: good for rolling out sugarpaste and other modelling pastes as it is portable and can be cleaned easily.

20 Non-stick rolling pins, large and small: it is well worth investing in a large, plastic rolling pin if you make a lot of cakes. If you are using a wooden rolling pin, make sure it is scrupulously clean before using it to roll out icing for a special-diet cake. Smaller rolling pins are used to roll small quantities of sugarpaste, modelling paste, flower paste or modelling chocolate for modelling or flowers.

21 Palette knife: a large, blunt knife used in cake making for spreading filling and lifting cakes. A small version with a cranked handle is useful for paddling royal icing and let-down sugarpaste (i.e. mixing with cooled, boiled water) to remove air bubbles and lumps.

22 Paper piping bags (not pictured): ideal for piping smaller designs. You can buy these ready-made or make your own from parchment paper (see page 105).

23 Scribing needle: a tool with a needle which is used for marking designs on cakes before adding decoration.

24 Small pointed scissors: for cutting into paste to give texture. Keep a pair for sugarcraft use only.

25 Turntable (not pictured): a tilted turntable is useful for decorating cakes as it avoids the need to handle them too much.

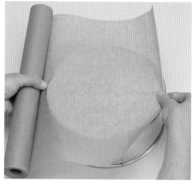  

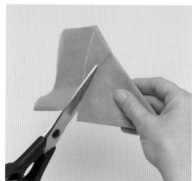 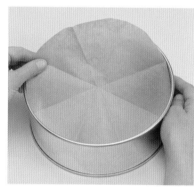 

Lining a Cake Tin

To line tins, I use baking parchment which is coated with silicone so it doesn't need greasing. It is also better for the environment as it can be composted, instead of being thrown away.

Round cake tins

1 Cut a square of baking parchment a little bigger than the cake tin. Fold the paper in half, then into quarters. Fold the paper over again to make a triangle with the centre of the paper as the point.

2 Turn the cake tin upside down and lay the triangle on top so that the point of the triangle is in the centre of the tin. Mark a line on the paper where it meets the side of the cake tin. Cut along this line, open the paper out and you should have a circle to line the base.

3 Cut strips of baking parchment to line the side of the cake tin, making sure there are no gaps.

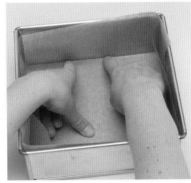

TOP TIP

For larger cakes, cut two squares of parchment and overlap them on a worktop. Place the cake tin centrally on top of the parchment and follow instructions below for lining a square cake tin to finish.

Square cake tins

1 Cut a square of baking parchment large enough to cover the bottom and the sides of the cake tin.

2 Place the cake tin centrally on top of the parchment. Make four cuts from the edge of the paper to the four corners of the tin.

3 Push the paper into the cake tin and fold the flaps at each corner around the back of the paper, lining the sides of the tin. Run your fingernail or a table knife along the inside edge of the tin to sharpen the edges of the paper.

Recipes

When baking a sponge celebration cake, I find it is best to cook it in two cake tins as this gives you a deeper cake. I aim to make the cake about 7.5cm (3") high when filled with jam and buttercream. Rich fruit cakes are baked in one tin.

All ovens are different so baking times are approximate. A cake is cooked when it has risen; the top should be firm and springy to the touch and when a knife is inserted into the centre it should come out clean.

The oven temperatures provided are based on a conventional oven. For fan ovens the temperature generally needs to be reduced by around 20°C, depending on the oven.

If recipes aren't already nut-free, alternatives are given to exclude any nuts. Remember to check the ingredient packaging before use to make sure it is suitable for your special diet.

LACTOSE- AND DAIRY-FREE CAKES

Here are my tips for best results:

To make a cake suitable for a dairy-free diet you can adapt your usual sponge cakes, replacing any butter in the recipe with dairy-free margarine or spread. There are now many dairy-free margarines available but they vary quite considerably in flavour and consistency, so it is worth testing a few to see which you prefer.

If a sponge recipe contains milk, this can be substituted with a dairy-free version such as sweetened soya milk (original), rice milk or almond milk (remember that these contain other allergens). If you are making a chocolate cake make sure any chocolate, cocoa and chocolate chips used are dairy-free. To make your cakes soya free also, check that none of the ingredients in the dairy-free margarine, dairy-free milk, chocolate and cocoa powder contains soya.

DAIRY-FREE

Vanilla Sponge Cake

Ingredients

300g (10oz) unrefined caster sugar

300g (10oz) dairy-free margarine

6 medium eggs

300g (10oz) self-raising flour

A few drops of vanilla extract

Filling

Jam of choice

For dairy-free vanilla buttercream, see Cake Fillings, page 88

Makes a 20cm (8") round cake or 18 large cupcakes

To make this recipe nut free, ensure the margarine is nut free.

TOP TIP

When making cupcakes I always use muffin cases; if you want to use small cupcake cases, divide this mixture in half and reduce the baking time. The cakes should rise to just below the top of the cake cases. .

1 Line two x 20cm (8") round cake tins with silicone-coated parchment paper (see page 28), or line with greaseproof paper and grease with sunflower oil or dairy-free margarine.

2 Preheat the oven to 190°C/375°F/gas mark 5.

3 Cream together the caster sugar and margarine until light and fluffy using a food mixer with a beater attachment or a hand-held electric mixer.

4 Crack the eggs into a bowl and beat lightly with a fork.

5 Beat the eggs into the creamed mixture a little at a time, making sure you beat in each addition well before adding the next. If the mixture starts to split, mix in a spoonful of the flour.

6 Add the vanilla extract.

7 Fold in the flour using a large metal spoon.

8 Divide the mixture equally between the two tins and bake for 20–25 minutes until firm to the touch or a knife inserted comes out clean.

9 Leave to cool in the tins for 5 minutes before turning out onto a cooling rack. Leave to cool completely before finishing with buttercream or any other decoration.

Variations

Lemon cake/cupcakes: add the zest of two lemons.

Chocolate cake/cupcakes: substitute 50g (2oz) of flour with cocoa powder.

Coffee cake/cupcakes: dissolve 2 heaped dessert spoons of coffee in 15ml (1tbsp) of boiling water and stir into the sponge mixture.

Quantities for a dairy-free vanilla sponge cake

ROUND	15cm (6")	20cm (8")	23cm (9")	25cm (10")	30cm (12")
Caster sugar	200g (7oz)	300g (10oz)	400g (14oz)	500g (1lb 1oz)	850g (1lb 13oz)
Dairy-free margarine	200g (7oz)	300g (10oz)	400g (14oz)	500g (1lb 1oz)	850g (1lb 13oz)
Eggs, medium	4	6	8	10	17
Self-raising flour	200g (7oz)	300g (10oz)	400g (14oz)	500g (1lb 1oz)	850g (1lb 13oz)
Divide into 2 tins and bake at 190°C/375°F/gas mark 5.	15–20 minutes	20–25 minutes	25–30 minutes	30–40 minutes	40–50 minutes

SQUARE	15cm (6")	20cm (8")	23cm (9")	25cm (10")	30cm (12")
Caster sugar	250g (9oz)	350g (12oz)	450g (1lb)	550g (1lb 3oz)	950g (2lb 1oz)
Dairy-free margarine	250g (9oz)	350g (12oz)	450g (1lb)	550g (1lb 3oz)	950g (2lb 1oz)
Eggs, medium	5	7	9	11	19
Self-raising flour	250g (9oz)	350g (12oz)	450g (1lb)	550g (1lb 3oz)	950g (2lb 1oz)
Divide into 2 tins and bake at 190°C/375°F/gas mark 5.	15–20 minutes	20–25 minutes	25–30 minutes	30–40 minutes	40–50 minutes

DAIRY-FREE
Rich Chocolate Cake

Ingredients

300g (10oz) dairy-free margarine

400g (14oz) caster sugar

90g (3¼oz) dairy-free plain chocolate

7 medium eggs

150g (5oz) self-raising flour

60g (2¼oz) dairy-free cocoa powder

75g (3oz) dairy-free chocolate chips, see Suppliers, page 168

Filling

Jam of choice

For dairy-free chocolate ganache, see Cake Fillings, page 84

Makes a 20cm (8") round cake or 18 large cupcakes

To make this recipe nut free, ensure the margarine, chocolate, cocoa powder and chocolate chips are nut free.

1 Line two x 20cm (8") round cake tins with silicone-coated parchment paper (see page 28), or line with greaseproof paper and grease with sunflower oil or dairy-free margarine.

2 Preheat the oven to 190°C/375°F/gas mark 5.

3 Cream together the dairy-free margarine and caster sugar until light and fluffy, using a food mixer with a beater attachment or a hand-held electric mixer. Melt the chocolate in the microwave on low, stirring every 30 seconds until melted, or over a bowl of just boiled water, making sure the base of the bowl does not come into contact with the water, or the chocolate may 'seize'.

4 Beat in the melted chocolate. Scrape down the bowl.

5 Crack the eggs into a bowl and beat lightly with a fork. Beat the eggs into the chocolate mixture a little at a time, making sure you beat in each addition fully before adding the next.

6 Sieve together the flour and cocoa powder and fold into the mixture, using a large metal spoon. Fold in the chocolate chips.

7 Divide the mixture between the cake tins and bake for 20–30 minutes until firm to the touch or a knife inserted comes out clean.

8 Leave to cool in the tins for 5 minutes, then turn out on to a cooling rack. Leave to cool before filling with jam and dairy-free chocolate ganache.

Quantities for a dairy-free rich chocolate cake

ROUND	15cm (6")	20cm (8")	23cm (9")	25cm (10")	30cm (12")
Self-raising flour	115g (4oz)	150g (5oz)	200g (7oz)	225g (8oz)	410g (14¼oz)
Dairy-free cocoa powder	45g (1¾oz)	65g (2½oz)	75g (3oz)	90g (3¼oz)	150g (5oz)
Caster sugar	340g (12oz)	395g (14oz)	650g (1lb 6oz)	675g (1lb 7oz)	1.35kg (2lb 15oz)
Dairy-free margarine	225g (8oz)	300g (10oz)	410g (14½oz)	450g (1lb)	825g (1lb 13oz)
Dairy-free plain chocolate (60% cocoa solids)	65g (2¼oz)	90g (3¼oz)	120g (4¼oz)	125g (4¼oz)	240g (8½oz)
Eggs, medium	5	7	9	10	19
Dairy-free chocolate chips	50g (2oz)	70g (2½oz)	85g (3oz)	100g (3½oz)	200g (7oz)
Divide into 2 tins and bake at 190°C/375°F/gas mark 5.	15–20 minutes	20–30 minutes	30–40 minutes	35–45 minutes	45 minutes–1 hour

SQUARE	15cm (6")	20cm (8")	23cm (9")	25cm (10")	30cm (12")
Self-raising flour	150g (5oz)	200g (7oz)	225g (8oz)	265g (9¼oz)	450g (1lb)
Dairy-free cocoa powder	60g (2¼oz)	75g (3oz)	90g (3¼oz)	105g (3½oz)	180g (6¼oz)
Caster sugar	395g (14oz)	650g (1lb 6oz)	675g (1lb 7oz)	775g (1lb 11oz)	1.35kg (2lb 15oz)
Dairy-free margarine	300g (10oz)	410g (14½oz)	450g (1lb)	525g (1lb 2½oz)	900g (2lb)
Dairy-free plain chocolate (60% cocoa solids)	90g (3¼oz)	120g (4oz)	125g (4oz)	150g (5oz)	250g (9oz)
Eggs, medium	7	9	10	12	20
Dairy-free chocolate chips	70g (3oz)	85g (3oz)	100g (3½oz)	135g (4¾oz)	200g (7oz)
Divide into 2 tins and bake at 190°C/375°F/gas mark 5.	15–20 minutes	20–30 minutes	30–40 minutes	35–45 minutes	45 minutes–1 hour

DAIRY-FREE

Carrot Cake

Ingredients

350g (12oz) self-raising flour

2tsp baking powder

2tsp mixed spice

½tsp salt

500g (1lb 1oz) carrots, grated

125g (4oz) raisins

300ml (10fl oz) sunflower oil

6 large eggs

350g (12oz) demerara sugar

A few drops of vanilla extract

Filling

For dairy-free orange buttercream, see Cake Fillings, page 88

Makes a 20cm (8") round cake

To make this recipe nut free, ensure the margarine is nut free.

1 Line two x 20cm (8") round cake tins with silicone-coated parchment paper (see page 28), or line with greaseproof paper and grease with sunflower oil or dairy-free margarine.

2 Preheat the oven to 180°C/350°F/gas mark 4.

3 Weigh the flour, baking powder, mixed spice and salt into a large bowl.

4 Add the grated carrot and raisins to the flour and stir together.

5 Measure the sunflower oil, eggs, demerara sugar and vanilla extract into a separate large mixing bowl. Whisk together until pale in colour then stir in the dry ingredients.

6 Pour into the prepared cake tins and bake for 40–50 minutes until firm to the touch, or until a knife inserted comes out clean.

7 Leave to cool in the tins for 5 minutes before turning out onto a cooling rack.

DAIRY-FREE

Lemon Cake

Ingredients

300g (10oz) dairy-free margarine

300g (10oz) caster sugar

6 medium eggs

300g (10oz) self-raising flour

Grated zest of 2 lemons

For the syrup:

300g (10oz) icing sugar

Juice of 2 lemons

Filling

For dairy-free lemon buttercream, see Cake Fillings, page 88

Makes a 20cm (8") round cake

To make this recipe nut free, ensure the margarine is nut free.

1 Line two 20cm (8") round cake tins with greaseproof paper and grease with sunflower oil or dairy-free margarine.

2 Preheat the oven to 190°C/375°F/gas mark 5.

3 Cream together the dairy-free margarine and caster sugar until light and fluffy, using a food mixer with a beater attachment or a hand-held electric mixer.

4 Crack the eggs into a bowl and beat lightly with a fork.

5 Beat the eggs into the creamed mixture a little at a time, making sure you beat in each addition fully before adding the next. If the mixture starts to split, mix in a spoonful of the flour.

6 Using a large metal spoon, fold in the flour with the grated lemon zest.

7 Divide the mixture equally between the cake tins and bake for 20–30 minutes until firm to the touch or a knife inserted comes out clean.

8 Leave to cool in the tin for 5 minutes before turning out onto a cooling rack.

9 When you are ready to fill the cake, place the icing sugar and lemon juice into a saucepan. Bring to the boil, stirring constantly.

10 Use a pastry brush to brush the syrup over each layer of cake before filling with dairy-free lemon buttercream.

DAIRY-FREE
Rich Fruit Cake

Ingredients

225g (8oz) currants

575g (1lb 4oz) sultanas

225g (8oz) raisins

75g (3oz) glacé cherries, chopped

75g (3oz) mixed peel, chopped

75ml (3fl oz) brandy, plus extra for spooning over the cake (optional)

275g (9¾oz) dairy-free margarine

175g (6oz) soft dark brown sugar

100g (3½oz) demerara or soft light brown sugar

5 large eggs

Zest of 1 lemon and orange

275g (9¾oz) plain flour

½tsp ground nutmeg

1tsp ground mixed spice

Makes a 20cm (8") round cake

To make this recipe nut free, ensure the margarine is nut free.

1 Place the currants, sultanas, raisins, cherries, mixed peel and brandy into a large bowl, cover and leave to soak overnight.

2 Line the cake tin with greaseproof paper (see page 28).

3 Preheat the oven to 150°C/300°F/gas mark 2.

4 Cream together the dairy-free margarine and both sugars until light and fluffy, using a food mixer with a beater attachment or a hand-held electric mixer.

5 Crack the eggs into a bowl and beat lightly with a fork.

6 Beat in the eggs.

7 Using a large metal spoon, fold in the soaked fruit, lemon and orange zest.

8 Fold in the flour with the nutmeg and mixed spice.

9 Spoon into the cake tin and use the back of a spoon or a pastry scraper to level the top. Cover the top of the cake with tin foil. Make a small hole in the centre of the foil for the steam to escape from.

10 Cut a piece of greaseproof paper long enough to wrap around the cake tin twice. Fold into four lengthways and wrap around the cake tin, securing with sticky tape.

11 Cut a piece of cardboard slightly bigger than the cake tin. Sit the cake tin on top. (Protecting the outside of the cake tin will prevent the cake from burning on the outside and keep it moist.) Cardboard is flammable so take extra care if using a gas oven.

12 Bake for 4–5 hours until the cake is firm to the touch or so that when you insert a knife it comes out clean.

13 Pour over more brandy when the cake is still warm (optional).

14 Leave the cake in the tin until it has completely cooled (this will keep the cake moist and help maintain its shape).

15 Wrap the cake in clean greaseproof paper and tin foil and store in a cool place until needed. It's important to wrap the cake in greaseproof paper first as tin foil alone will react with the acid in the fruit. This cake is best left to mature for two months before serving.

Quantities for a dairy-free rich fruit cake

ROUND	15cm (6")	20cm (8")	23cm (9")	25cm (10")	30cm (12")
SQUARE	13cm (5")	18cm (7")	20cm (8")	23cm (9")	30cm (12")
Currants	110g (4oz)	225g (8oz)	285g (10oz)	350g (12oz)	575g (1lb 4oz)
Raisins	110g (4oz)	225g (8oz)	285g (10oz)	350g (12oz)	575g (1lb 4oz)
Sultanas	335g (11¾oz)	575g (1lb 4oz)	750g (1lb 10½oz)	900g (2lb)	1.5kg (3lb 5oz)
Mixed peel	60g (2¼oz)	75g (3oz)	85g (3oz)	110g (4oz)	170g (6oz)
Glacé cherries	60g (2¼oz)	75g (3oz)	85g (3oz)	110g (4oz)	170g (6oz)
Brandy	60ml (2¼fl oz)	75ml (3fl oz)	85ml (3fl oz)	110ml (4fl oz)	170ml (6fl oz)
Dairy-free margarine	165g (5¾oz)	275g (9¾oz)	350g (12oz)	450g (1lb)	750g (1lb 10½oz)
Dark brown sugar	85g (3oz)	140g (4¾oz)	175g (6oz)	225g (8oz)	375g (13¼oz)
Demerara sugar	80g (3oz)	135g (4¾oz)	175g (6oz)	225g (8oz)	375g (13¼oz)
Eggs, medium	3	5	7	9	13
Self-raising flour	165g (5¾oz)	275g (9¾oz)	350g (12oz)	450g (1lb)	750g (1lb 10½oz)
Mixed spice	½tsp	¾tsp	1tsp	1½tsp	2tsp
Ground nutmeg	¼tsp	½tsp	½tsp	¾tsp	1tsp
Bake at 150°C/300°F/gas mark 2.	3–3½ hours	4–5 hours	5–5½ hours	5½–6½ hours	8½–9 hours

WHEAT- AND GLUTEN-FREE CAKES

Here are my tips for best results:

These gluten-free cake recipes and the nut-free and dairy-free versions are at their best for about five days.

In all recipes requiring self-raising gluten-free flour, I advise sieving the flours together with the gluten-free baking powder four times to make sure all the ingredients are evenly distributed. If, in the past, you have made a cake that was really heavy with a solid lump of eggy mixture at the bottom, one reason could be that the baking powder wasn't mixed into the flour properly.

If you can't find maize flour, cornflour is readily available and makes a good substitute. There isn't much difference but I prefer maize flour. When baking pastry and biscuits, gram

(chickpea) flour is just as good as maize flour and is easily available. You may need to use more gram flour in the recipes.

Gluten-free sponge cakes are best eaten fresh. They can be frozen but the texture becomes a little grainy when defrosted.

As gluten-free cake is crumblier than others, use a sharp, serrated knife to carefully saw through it. Avoid pushing the knife into the cake too hard.

Use a flat baking tray to help move the layers of cooked sponge and save them from breaking. Turn the cake out from the tin onto a plate first and then onto a cooling rack. This will ensure the cake cools the right way up and prevents it from breaking in half.

WHEAT- AND GLUTEN-FREE
Vanilla Sponge Cake

Ingredients

150g (5oz) gluten-free plain flour

75g (3oz) maize flour or cornflour

75g (3oz) ground almonds

1½tsp gluten-free baking powder

300g (10oz) unrefined caster sugar

300g (10oz) butter, at room temperature

6 medium eggs

A few drops of vanilla extract

Filling

For vanilla buttercream, see Cake Fillings, page 87

Makes a 20cm (8") round cake or 18 large cupcakes

1 Line two 20cm (8") round cake tins with silicone-coated parchment paper (see page 28), or line with greaseproof paper and grease with sunflower oil or dairy-free margarine.

2 Preheat the oven to 190°C/375°F/gas mark 5.

3 Combine the gluten-free flour, maize flour, ground almonds and gluten-free baking powder. Sieve together four times to distribute all of the ingredients fully (see note on page 43).

4 Cream together the caster sugar and butter until light and fluffy. It is best to do this using a food mixer with a beater attachment or use a hand-held electric mixer.

5 Crack the eggs into a bowl and beat lightly with a fork.

6 Beat the eggs into the creamed mixture a little at a time, making sure you beat in each addition fully before adding the next. If the mixture starts to split, stir in a spoonful of the flour mixture.

7 Add the vanilla extract. Using a large metal spoon, fold in the gluten-free flour mixture.

8 Divide the mixture between the tins and bake for 20–25 minutes until firm to the touch or a knife inserted comes out clean.

9 Leave to cool in the tin for 15 minutes before turning out onto a plate then onto a cooling rack.

TOP TIP

When making cupcakes I always use muffin cases, but if you want to use small cupcake cases then divide this mixture in half and reduce the baking time. The cakes should rise to just below the top of the cake cases. Cupcakes are at their best only for a day or two.

Variations

To make this recipe nut free, use 300g (10oz) Doves Farm self-raising gluten-free flour in place of the gluten-free flour, maize flour, ground almond and gluten-free baking powder mixture. Skip step 3 of the recipe. Ensure the margarine is nut free.

To make this recipe dairy free, use dairy-free margarine in place of butter in the sponge and fill with jam and dairy-free buttercream (see page 88).

Lemon cake/cupcakes: add the zest of two lemons.

Chocolate cake/cupcakes: substitute 50g (2oz) of maize flour with cocoa powder.

Coffee cake/cupcakes: dissolve 2 heaped dessert spoons of coffee in 15ml (1tbsp) of boiling water and stir into the sponge mixture.

Quantities for a wheat- and gluten-free vanilla sponge cake

ROUND	15cm (6")	20cm (8")	23cm (9")	25cm (10")	30cm (12")
Caster sugar	200g (7oz)	300g (10oz)	400g (14oz)	500g (1lb 1oz)	850g (1lb 13oz)
Butter or margarine	200g (7oz)	300g (10oz)	400g (14oz)	500g (1lb 1oz)	850g (1lb 13oz)
Eggs, medium	4	6	8	10	17
Gluten-free plain flour	100g (3½oz)	150g (5oz)	200g (7oz)	250g (9oz)	425g (15oz)
Maize flour/ cornflour	50g (2oz)	75g (3oz)	100g (3½oz)	125g (4oz)	212g (7½oz)
Ground almonds	50g (2oz)	75g (3oz)	100g (3½oz)	125g (4oz)	213g (7½oz)
Gluten-free baking powder	1tsp	1½tsp	2tsp	2½tsp	4½tsp
Bake at 190°C/375°F/gas mark 5. Divide into 2 tins.	15–20 minutes	20–25 minutes	25–30 minutes	30–40 minutes	40–50 minutes

SQUARE	15cm (6")	20cm (8")	23cm (9")	25cm (10")	30cm (12")
Caster sugar	250g (9oz)	350g (12oz)	450g (1lb)	550g (1lb 3oz)	950g (2lb 1oz)
Dairy-free margarine	250g (9oz)	350g (12oz)	450g (1lb)	550g (1lb 3½oz)	950g (2lb 1oz)
Eggs, medium	5	7	9	11	19
Gluten-free plain flour	125g (4oz)	175g (6oz)	225g (8oz)	275g (9¾oz)	475g (1lb ¾oz)
Maize flour/ cornflour	60g (2¼oz)	85g (3¼oz)	110g (4oz)	135g (4¾oz)	235g (8¼oz)
Ground almonds	65g (2¼oz)	90g (3¼oz)	115g (4oz)	140g (4¾oz)	240g (8¼oz)
Gluten-free baking powder	1¼tsp	1¾tsp	2¼tsp	2¾tsp	4¾tsp
Bake at 190°C/375°F/gas mark 5. Divide into 2 tins.	15–20 minutes	20–25 minutes	25–30 minutes	30–40 minutes	40–50 minutes

WHEAT- AND GLUTEN-FREE
Rich Chocolate Cake

Ingredients

150g (5oz) gluten-free plain flour

1tsp gluten-free baking powder

60g (2¼oz) gluten-free cocoa powder

90g (3¼oz) gluten-free plain chocolate (60% cocoa solids)

300g (10oz) butter or margarine, at room temperature

390g (13oz) caster sugar

7 medium eggs

75g (3oz) gluten-free chocolate chips, see Suppliers, page 168

Filling

For chocolate ganache, see Cake Fillings, page 82

Makes a 20cm (8") round cake

1 Line two 20cm (8") round cake tins with silicone-coated parchment paper (see page 28), or line with greaseproof paper and grease with sunflower oil or dairy-free margarine.

2 Preheat the oven to 190°C/375°F/ gas mark 5.

3 Sieve the gluten-free plain flour, gluten-free baking powder and cocoa powder together four times.

4 Melt the chocolate on a low heat in a microwave, stirring every 30 seconds until melted. Alternatively, melt over a bowl of just boiled water, making sure the base of the bowl does not come into contact with the water, otherwise the chocolate may 'seize'.

5 Cream together the butter and caster sugar using a food mixer with

a beater attachment or a hand-held electric mixer.

6 Beat in the slightly cooled, melted chocolate. Scrape down the bowl.

7 Crack the eggs into a bowl and beat lightly with a fork.

8 Beat the eggs into the chocolate mixture.

9 Using a large metal spoon, fold in the flour mixture along with the chocolate chips.

10 Divide the mixture between the cake tins and bake for 20–30 minutes until firm to the touch or a knife inserted comes out clean.

11 Leave to cool in the cake tin for 10 minutes before turning out onto a plate then a cooling rack.

TOP TIP

I find using margarine rather than butter in this recipe produces a moister cake.

Variations

Try using the same quantity of ground hazelnuts in place of gluten-free flour and dried fruit or nuts in place of the chocolate chips. **CONTAINS NUTS.**

To make this recipe dairy free, use dairy-free margarine in place of butter and dairy- and gluten-free plain chocolate. Use gluten- and dairy-free cocoa powder and chocolate chips (see Suppliers, page 168).

Quantities for a wheat- and gluten-free rich chocolate cake

ROUND	15cm (6")	20cm (8")	23cm (9")	25cm (10")	30cm (12")
Gluten-free plain flour	115g (4oz)	150g (5oz)	200g (7oz)	225g (8oz)	410g (14¼oz)
Gluten-free cocoa powder	45g (1¾oz)	65g (2½oz)	75g (3oz)	90g (3¼oz)	150g (5oz)
Gluten-free baking powder	¾tsp	1tsp	1½tsp	1½tsp	1tbsp
Caster sugar	340g (12oz)	395g (14oz)	650g (1lb 6oz)	675g (1lb 7oz)	1.35kg (2lb 15oz)
Butter or margarine	225g (8oz)	300g (10oz)	410g (14½oz)	450g (1lb)	825g (1lb 13oz)
Gluten-free plain chocolate (60% cocoa solids)	65g (2¼oz)	90g (3¼oz)	120g (4¼oz)	125g (4¼oz)	240g (8½oz)
Eggs, medium	5	7	9	10	19
Gluten-free chocolate chips	50g (2oz)	70g (2½oz)	85g (3oz)	100g (3½oz)	200g (7oz)
Divide into 2 tins and bake at 190°C/375°F/gas mark 5.	15–20 minutes	20–30 minutes	30–40 minutes	35–45 minutes	45 minutes–1 hour

SQUARE	15cm (6")	20cm (8")	23cm (9")	25cm (10")	30cm (12")
Gluten-free plain flour	150g (5oz)	200g (7oz)	225g (8oz)	265g (9¼oz)	450g (1lb)
Gluten-free cocoa powder	60g (2¼oz)	75g (3oz)	90g (3¼oz)	105g (3½oz)	180g (6¼oz)
Gluten-free baking powder	1tsp	1½tsp	1½tsp	1¾tsp	3¼tsp
Caster sugar	395g (14oz)	650g (1lb 6oz)	675g (1lb 7oz)	775g (1lb 11oz)	1.35kg (2lb 15oz)
Butter or margarine	300g (10oz)	410g (14½oz)	450g (1lb)	525g (1lb 2½oz)	900g (2lb)
Gluten-free plain chocolate (60% cocoa solids)	90g (3¼oz)	120g (4oz)	125g (4oz)	150g (5oz)	250g (9oz)
Eggs, medium	7	9	10	12	20
Gluten-free chocolate chips	70g (3oz)	85g (3oz)	100g (3½oz)	135g (4¾oz)	200g (7oz)
Divide into 2 tins and bake at 190°C/375°F/gas mark 5.	15–20 minutes	20–30 minutes	30–40 minutes	35–45 minutes	45 minutes–1 hour

WHEAT- AND GLUTEN-FREE

Ingredients

150g (5oz) gluten-free plain flour

75g (3oz) maize flour or cornflour

75g (3oz) ground almonds

1½tsp gluten-free baking powder

300g (10oz) butter or margarine, at room temperature

300g (10oz) unrefined caster sugar

6 medium eggs

Grated zest of 2 lemons

For the syrup:

300g (10oz) icing sugar

Juice of 2 lemons

Filling

For lemon buttercream, see Cake Fillings, page 87

Makes a 20cm (8") round cake

1 Grease and line two 20cm (8") round cake tins with greaseproof paper or silicone-coated parchment paper (see page 28).

2 Preheat the oven to 190°C/375°F/gas mark 5.

3 Sieve together the gluten-free flour, maize flour, ground almonds and gluten-free baking powder four times.

4 Cream together the butter and caster sugar until light and fluffy, using a food mixer with a beater attachment or a hand-held electric mixer.

5 Lightly beat the eggs, then beat them into the creamed mixture a little at a time, making sure you beat in each addition fully before adding the next. If the mixture starts to split, mix in a spoonful of the flour.

6 Fold in the flour mixture, along with the grated lemon zest.

7 Divide the mixture equally between the cake tins and bake for 20–30 minutes until firm to the touch or a knife inserted comes out clean.

8 Leave to cool in the tin for 15 minutes before turning out onto a plate then onto a cooling rack.

9 When you are ready to fill the cake, make the lemon syrup. Place the icing sugar and the lemon juice in a saucepan and, whilst stirring, bring to the boil.

10 Use a pastry brush to brush the syrup over each layer of cake before filling with lemon buttercream.

Variations

To make this recipe nut free, use 300g (10oz) Doves Farm self-raising gluten-free flour in place of the gluten-free flour, maize flour, ground almond and gluten-free baking powder mixture. Skip step 3 of the recipe. Ensure the margarine is nut free.

To make this recipe dairy free, use dairy-free margarine in place of butter. Fill with dairy-free buttercream flavoured with the grated zest of one lemon (see page 88).

WHEAT- AND GLUTEN-FREE
Carrot Cake

Ingredients

175g (6oz) gluten-free plain flour

85g (3oz) maize flour or cornflour

90g (3¼oz) ground almonds

4tsp gluten-free baking powder

3tsp mixed spice

½tsp salt

500g (1lb 1oz) carrots, grated

120g (4oz) raisins

300ml (10fl oz) sunflower oil

6 large eggs

350g (12oz) demerara sugar

A few drops of vanilla extract

Filling

For orange buttercream, see Cake
Fillings, page 87

Makes a 20cm (8") round cake

1 Line two x 20cm (8") round cake tins
with silicone-coated parchment paper
(see page 28), or line with greaseproof
paper and grease with sunflower oil or
dairy-free margarine.

2 Preheat the oven to 180°C/350°F/gas
mark 4.

3 Combine the gluten-free flour, maize
flour, ground almonds, baking powder,
mixed spice and salt in a bowl. Sieve
together four times.

4 Add the grated carrot and raisins to
the flour and stir together.

Variation

To make this recipe nut free, use 300g (10oz) Doves Farm self-raising gluten-free
flour in place of the gluten-free flour, maize flour, ground almond and gluten-free
baking powder mixture. Skip step 3 of the recipe.

5 Measure the sunflower oil, eggs,
brown sugar and vanilla extract into
a large mixing bowl. Whisk together
until pale in colour then stir in the dry
ingredients.

6 Pour into the prepared cake tins and
bake for 40–50 minutes until firm to the
touch or a knife inserted comes out
clean.

7 Leave to cool in the tins for 15
minutes before turning out onto a plate
then onto a cooling rack.

*This sponge is dairy free and can be
filled with dairy-free orange buttercream
(see page 88).*

WHEAT- AND GLUTEN-FREE
Rich Fruit Cake

Ingredients

225g (8oz) currants

575g (1lb 4¼oz) sultanas

225g (8oz) raisins

75g (3oz) wheat-free glacé cherries, chopped

75g (3oz) wheat-free mixed peel, chopped

75ml (3fl oz) brandy, plus extra to feed the cake (optional)

275g (9¾oz) unsalted butter or margarine, at room temperature

140g (4¾oz) soft dark brown sugar

135g (4¾oz) demerara sugar

5 large eggs

Zest of 1 lemon and orange

140g (4¾oz) gluten-free plain flour

70g (2¾oz) maize flour or cornflour

65g (2½oz) ground almonds

½tsp ground nutmeg

1tsp ground mixed spice

Makes a 20cm (8") round cake

1 Place the currants, sultanas, raisins, cherries, mixed peel and brandy into a large bowl, cover and leave to soak overnight.

2 Line the cake tin with greaseproof paper or silicone-coated parchment paper (see page 28).

3 Preheat the oven to 150°C/300°F/ gas mark 2.

4 Cream together the butter and sugars until light and fluffy using a food mixer with a beater attachment or a hand-held electric mixer.

5 Lightly beat the eggs, then add them to the butter and sugar mixture.

6 Fold in the soaked fruit, lemon and orange zest.

7 Sieve together the gluten-free flour, maize flour, ground almonds, nutmeg and mixed spice and fold into the mixture.

8 Spoon into the cake tin and use the back of a spoon or pastry scraper to level the top. Cover the top of the cake with tin foil. Make a small hole in the centre.

9 Cut a piece of greaseproof paper long enough to wrap around the cake tin twice. Fold into four lengthways and wrap around the cake tin, securing with sticky tape.

10 Cut a piece of cardboard slightly bigger than the cake tin. Sit the cake tin on top. Cardboard is flammable so take extra care if using a gas oven.

11 Bake for 4–5 hours until a knife inserted comes out clean.

12 Pour over more brandy when the cake is still warm (optional).

13 Leave the cake in the tin until it is cold, which will ensure it stays moist and retains its shape.

14 Wrap the cake in clean greaseproof paper and tin foil and store in a cool place until needed. It's important to first wrap in greaseproof paper as tin foil alone will react with the acid in the fruit. The cake is better if left to mature for two months before serving.

Variations

To make this recipe nut free, use 300g (10oz) Doves Farm plain gluten-free flour in place of the gluten-free flour, maize flour and ground almond mixture. Ensure the margarine is nut free.

To make this recipe dairy free, use dairy-free margarine in place of butter.

Quantities for a wheat- and gluten-free rich fruit cake

ROUND	15cm (6")	20cm (8")	23cm (9")	25cm (10")	30cm (12")
SQUARE	13cm (5")	18cm (7")	20cm (8")	23cm (9")	30cm (12")
Currants	110g (4oz)	225g (8oz)	285g (10oz)	350g (12oz)	575g (1lb 4oz)
Raisins	110g (4oz)	225g (8oz)	285g (10oz)	350g (12oz)	575g (1lb 4oz)
Sultanas	335g (11¾oz)	575g (1lb 4oz)	750g (1lb 10½oz)	900g (2lb)	1.5kg (3lb 5oz)
Mixed peel	60g (2¼oz)	75g (3oz)	85g (3oz)	110g (4oz)	170g (6oz)
Glacé cherries	60g (2¼oz)	75g (3oz)	85g (3oz)	110g (4oz)	170g (6oz)
Brandy	60ml (2¼fl oz)	75ml (3fl oz)	85ml (3fl oz)	110ml (4fl oz)	170ml (6fl oz)
Butter	165g (5¾oz)	275g (9¾oz)	350g (12oz)	450g (1lb)	750g (1lb 10½oz)
Dark brown sugar	85g (3oz)	140g (4¾oz)	175g (6oz)	225g (8oz)	375g (13¼oz)
Demerara sugar	80g (3oz)	135g (4¾oz)	175g (6oz)	225g (8oz)	375g (13¼oz)
Eggs, medium	3	5	7	9	13
Gluten-free plain flour	85g (3oz)	140g (4¾oz)	175g (6oz)	225g (8oz)	375g (13¼oz)
Maize flour	40g (1½oz)	70g (2½oz)	90g (3¼oz)	115g (4oz)	185g (6¼oz)
Ground almonds	40g (1½oz)	65g (2¼oz)	85g (3oz)	110g (4oz)	190g (6¾oz)
Mixed spice	½tsp	¾tsp	1tsp	1½tsp	2tsp
Ground nutmeg	¼tsp	½tsp	½tsp	¾tsp	1tsp
Bake at 150°C/300°F/gas mark 2.	3–3½ hours	4–5 hours	5–5½ hours	5½–6½ hours	8½–9 hours

WHEAT- AND GLUTEN-FREE

Chocolate, Rum and Raisin Fruit Cake

Ingredients

1.25kg (2lb 4¼oz) raisins

125ml (4fl oz) dark rum, plus extra for 'feeding' the cake (optional)

275g (9¾oz) unsalted butter

275g (9¾oz) demerara sugar

150g (5oz) gluten-free plain chocolate

5 medium eggs

Zest of 2 oranges (optional)

125g (4oz) gluten-free plain flour

40g (1½oz) maize flour or cornflour

60g (2¼oz) ground almonds

50g (2oz) gluten-free cocoa powder

Makes a 20cm (8") round cake

Variations

To make this recipe nut free, use 225g (8oz) Doves Farm plain gluten-free flour and 50g (1¾oz) gluten-free cocoa powder sieved together in place of the gluten-free flour, maize flour, ground almond and cocoa mixture. Ensure the margarine and chocolate are nut free.

To make this recipe dairy free, replace the butter with dairy-free margarine. Ensure the plain chocolate is dairy-free.

1 Place the raisins and rum in a large bowl, cover and leave to soak overnight.

2 Line the cake tin with greaseproof paper or silicone-coated parchment paper (see page 28).

3 Preheat the oven to 150°C/300°F/gas mark 2.

4 Cream together the butter and sugar until light and fluffy.

5 Melt the chocolate in the microwave on low, stirring every 30 seconds until melted, or in a bowl over a pan of just boiled water, making sure the base of the bowl does not come into contact with the water or the chocolate may 'seize'.

6 Mix the slightly cooled, melted chocolate into the creamed mixture. Scrape down the sides of the bowl and mix again.

7 Lightly beat the eggs, then beat them into the chocolate mixture.

8 Fold in the soaked raisins and orange zest, if using.

9 Sieve together the gluten-free flour, maize flour, ground almonds and cocoa powder and, using a large metal spoon, fold into the mixture.

10 Spoon into the cake tin and use the back of a spoon or a pastry scraper to level the top. Cover the top of the cake with tin foil. Make a small hole in the centre.

11 Cut a piece of greaseproof paper long enough to wrap around the cake tin twice. Fold into four lengthways, wrap around the cake tin and secure with sticky tape.

12 Cut a piece of cardboard slightly bigger than the cake tin. Sit the cake tin on top. Cardboard is flammable so take extra care if using a gas oven.

13 Bake for 4–5 hours until a knife inserted comes out clean.

14 Pour over more rum when the cake is still warm (optional).

15 Leave the cake in the tin until it is cold, which will ensure it stays moist and retains its shape.

16 Wrap in clean greaseproof paper and tin foil and store in a cool place until needed. The cake is best if left to mature for two months before serving.

WHEAT- AND GLUTEN-FREE

Banana and Chocolate Chunk Cake

Ingredients

150g (5oz) gluten-free plain flour

75g (3oz) maize flour or cornflour

75g (3oz) ground almonds

1½tsp gluten-free baking powder

300g (10oz) butter or margarine, at room temperature

300g (10½oz) unrefined caster sugar

6 medium eggs

2 small ripe bananas, mashed

60g (2¼oz) gluten-free plain chocolate, cut into chunks

A few drops of vanilla extract

Filling

For vanilla buttercream, see Cake Fillings, page 87

Makes a 20cm (8") round cake

1 Preheat the oven to 190°C/375°F/gas mark 5.

2 Grease and line two 20cm (8") round cake tins with greaseproof paper or silicone-coated parchment paper (see page 28).

3 Sieve together the gluten-free flour, maize flour, ground almonds and gluten-free baking powder four times.

4 Cream together the butter and caster sugar, using a food mixer with a beater attachment or a hand-held electric mixer.

5 Lightly beat the eggs, then beat them into the mixture a little at a time, adding a spoonful of the flour if the mixture looks as if it may split.

6 Fold in the mashed banana, chocolate chunks and vanilla extract, then fold in the flour mixture using a large metal spoon.

7 Divide the mixture between the cake tins, level the top and bake for 25–30 minutes until firm to the touch or a knife inserted comes out clean. If the top of the cake browns before the cake is cooked, place a piece of greaseproof paper over the top and put back into the oven until it is fully baked.

8 Leave the cake to cool in the tins for 15 minutes before turning out onto a plate then onto a cooling rack.

Variations

To make this recipe nut free, use 300g (10oz) Doves Farm self-raising gluten-free flour in place of the gluten-free flour, maize flour, ground almond and gluten-free baking powder mixture. Skip step 3 of the recipe. Ensure the margarine is nut free.

To make this recipe dairy free, use dairy-free margarine in place of the butter in the cake and dairy- and gluten-free plain chocolate. Fill with dairy-free buttercream (see page 88).

WHEAT- AND GLUTEN-FREE

Coffee and Walnut Cake

Ingredients

150g (5oz) gluten-free plain flour

75g (3oz) maize flour or cornflour

75g (3oz) walnuts, ground (you can use a food processor or coffee grinder to do this)

1½tsp gluten-free baking powder

300g (10oz) butter or margarine, at room temperature

300g (10oz) unrefined caster sugar

6 medium eggs

1½tbsp instant coffee granules, diluted with a tiny amount of boiling water

A handful of chopped walnuts

Filling

For coffee buttercream, see Cake Fillings, page 87

Makes a 20cm (8") round cake

1 Preheat the oven to 190°C/375°F/gas mark 5.

2 Grease and line two 20cm (8") round cake tins with greaseproof paper or silicone-coated parchment paper (see page 28).

3 Sieve together the gluten-free flour, maize flour, ground walnuts and gluten-free baking powder four times to incorporate the baking powder fully.

4 Cream the butter and sugar together, using a food mixer with a beater attachment or a hand-held electric mixer.

5 Crack the eggs into a bowl and beat lightly, then beat them into the creamed mixture a little at a time. If the mixture looks as if it is going to split, fold in a spoonful of the flour.

6 Using a large metal spoon, fold in the flour mixture and the diluted coffee.

7 Fold in the chopped walnut pieces.

8 Divide the mixture between the two cake tins and level the top.

9 Bake for 25–35 minutes until firm to the touch or a knife inserted comes out clean.

10 Leave to cool in the tin for 15 minutes before turning out onto a plate then onto a cooling rack.

Variations

To make this recipe nut free, use 300g (10oz) Doves Farm self-raising gluten-free flour in place of the gluten-free flour, maize flour, ground walnut and gluten-free baking powder mixture. Omit the chopped walnuts from the ingredients. Skip step 3 of the recipe.

To make this recipe dairy free, use dairy-free margarine in place of butter in the sponge.

WHEAT- AND GLUTEN-FREE
Coconut Cake

Ingredients

150g (5oz) gluten-free plain flour

50g (2oz) maize flour or cornflour

50g (2oz) ground almonds

1½tsp gluten-free baking powder

50g (2oz) desiccated coconut

1 x 50g (2oz) sachet creamed coconut

300g (10oz) butter or margarine, at room temperature

300g (10oz) unrefined caster sugar

6 medium eggs

A few drops of vanilla extract

Filling

For vanilla buttercream, see Cake Fillings (page 87)

Makes a 20cm (8") round cake

1 Preheat the oven to 190°C/375°F/gas mark 5.

2 Grease and line two 20cm (8") round cake tins with greaseproof paper or silicone-coated parchment paper (see page 28).

3 Sieve together the gluten-free flour, maize flour, ground almonds and gluten-free baking powder four times to ensure the baking powder is fully incorporated. Stir in the desiccated coconut.

4 Place the unopened sachet of creamed coconut into a mug and pour enough boiling water over the coconut to melt it.

5 Cream together the butter and caster sugar until light and fluffy, using a food mixer with a beater attachment or a hand-held electric mixer.

6 Lightly beat the eggs then beat them into the mixture a little at a time with the vanilla extract. If the mixture looks as if it is going to split, fold in a spoonful of the flour.

7 Stir in the melted creamed coconut.

8 Using a large metal spoon, fold in the flour and desiccated coconut mixture.

9 Divide the mixture between the cake tins, level the top of the cakes and bake for 20–25 minutes until firm to the touch or a knife inserted comes out clean.

10 Leave to cool in the tin for 15 minutes before turning out onto a plate then onto a cooling rack.

Variations

Some people who are allergic to nuts find they can eat coconut. If you are able to eat coconut and you want to make this recipe nut free, use 250g (9oz) Doves Farm self-raising gluten-free flour in place of the gluten-free flour, maize flour and ground almond mixture, then stir in 50g (2oz) desiccated coconut. Skip step 3 of the recipe. Note that coconut can sometimes be contaminated with nuts during processing so always check the label.

To make this recipe dairy free, use dairy-free margarine in place of butter in the sponge and fill with dairy-free buttercream (see page 88).

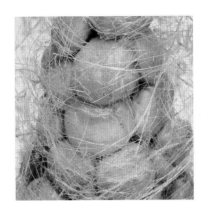

WHEAT- AND GLUTEN-FREE
Choux Pastry

Ingredients

50g (2oz) butter

125ml (4½fl oz) water

Salt and sugar

65g (2½oz) gluten-free plain flour

2 medium eggs, beaten

This gluten-free choux pastry works and tastes just like choux pastry made with wheat flour. I make this pastry for everyone and people do not realise it is gluten-free.

1 Cut the butter into small pieces. Put into a saucepan with 125ml (4fl oz) of water and a pinch of salt and sugar.

2 Bring the water to the boil. The butter should have melted by the time the water boils.

3 Turn off the heat and quickly stir in the gluten-free flour: one method of doing this is to fold a piece of greaseproof paper into a cone and 'shoot' the flour into the pan. Place back on the heat and beat briskly with a wooden spoon for 20 seconds.

4 Leave to cool until you can comfortably handle the mixture.

5 Beat in the egg a little at a time until the mixture just falls off the spoon when lifted. It may not be necessary to use all the egg and the pastry will not rise properly if too much is added.

Use this recipe to make profiteroles for a croquembouche (see page 134).

Variations

To make this recipe dairy free, use Vitalite® dairy-free spread in place of butter. Other dairy-free spreads and margarines will also work but the choux buns may not rise as well.

To make this recipe nut free, ensure the margarine is nut free.

WHEAT- AND GLUTEN-FREE

Ingredients

Wheat- and gluten-free choux pastry
(see page 59 for recipe)

Filling

Whipped cream or pastry cream, see
Cake Fillings, page 90

Makes approximately 24 profiteroles

Variations

If you are following the dairy-free recipe
(see page 59), fill the profiteroles with
dairy-free pastry cream or whipped
soya cream. Soya cream suitable for
whipping is available from health or
whole food shops.

1 Preheat the oven to 220°C/425°F/
gas mark 7.

2 Line a baking tray with greaseproof
paper and brush with oil.

3 Put a large, plain piping nozzle in
a nylon piping bag and fill with the
wheat- and gluten-free choux pastry.

4 Pipe approximately 24 small balls
on the tray, spaced evenly apart. Try to
pipe them all the same size.

5 Place in the oven and bake for
20–25 minutes. Check the profiteroles
during cooking: if they are browning
too much, the tray may need turning
around or placing on a lower shelf to
finish cooking. They are cooked when
no white part can be seen near the
bottom of the pastry. If using a gas
oven it may be necessary to pierce a

hole in each profiterole and continue
cooking for another 5–10 minutes with
the oven door slightly open. This is
because there is more moisture in a
gas oven.

6 Allow to cool completely.

TOP TIP

The profiteroles can be
frozen at this stage until
needed. When defrosting,
take out of the freezer
bag and leave at room
temperature. They will
defrost in a few minutes.

7 To serve, fit a nylon piping bag
with a small plain nozzle then fill it
with whipped cream or pastry cream
(page 90). Push the nozzle into each
profiterole and fill with the cream.

WHEAT- AND GLUTEN-FREE
Shortbread

Ingredients

70g (2½oz) caster sugar

140g (4¾oz) unsalted butter, at room temperature

100g (3½oz) gluten-free plain flour

100g (3½oz) maize flour

Makes 12 x 7.5cm (3") round biscuits

1 Preheat the oven to 180°C/350°F/gas mark 4.

2 Cream the sugar and butter together until light and fluffy, using a food mixer with a beater attachment or a hand-held electric mixer.

3 Mix in the gluten-free flour and maize flour and bring together to form a dough.

4 Roll out to 5mm (¼") thick and press out shapes using biscuit cutters.

5 Place onto a baking tray lined with greaseproof paper and brushed with oil, or lined with silicone-coated parchment paper.

6 Bake for 8 minutes for small biscuits and 13–15 minutes for larger biscuits. Leave on the baking tray to cool. Decorate as required. For decoration ideas see Animal Sugar Biscuits or Shortbread on page 110.

Variations

To make this recipe dairy free, use dairy-free margarine in place of butter.

For nutty shortbread, try substituting 100g (3½oz) maize flour with 100g (3½oz) ground hazelnuts and continue as above. **CONTAINS NUTS.**

TOP TIP

Shortbread is a great base for a range of desserts and biscuits. Gluten-free biscuits are quite fragile, so be gentle when lifting.

WHEAT- AND GLUTEN-FREE

Ingredients

100g (3½oz) unsalted butter

75g (3oz) dark brown sugar

50g (2oz) golden syrup

100g (3½oz) maize flour

100g (3½oz) gluten-free plain flour

1tsp gluten-free baking powder

1tsp mixed spice

2tsp ground ginger

Makes 14–16 biscuits

TOP TIP

When making large gingerbread biscuits, roll the dough slightly thicker to add strength as gluten-free dough is quite fragile.

1 In a saucepan melt together the butter, dark brown sugar and golden syrup. Leave to cool slightly.

2 Sieve together the maize flour, gluten-free flour, baking powder, mixed spice and ground ginger.

3 Stir into the melted ingredients to form a dough. If it looks too runny leave it to cool before rolling out.

4 Line a baking tray with greaseproof paper and brush with oil, or line with silicone-coated parchment paper.

5 Preheat the oven to 180°C/350°F/gas mark 4.

6 Dust the worktop with gluten-free flour and roll out the gingerbread to 5mm (¼") thick.

7 Cut out shapes using biscuit cutters. Lift away the excess gingerbread dough and transfer the biscuits to the baking tray with a palette knife or pastry scraper.

8 Roll out the leftover dough and cut out more biscuits. Do this until you have used up all of the dough.

9 Bake for 12–15 minutes until golden-brown. Leave to cool on the baking tray.

10 When nearly cold, run a palette knife underneath to loosen the gingerbread from the greaseproof/ parchment paper.

11 Decorate as required. For decoration ideas see Christmas Gingerbread on page 113.

Variations

To make this recipe dairy free and vegan, use dairy-free margarine in place of butter.

To make this recipe nut free, ensure the margarine is nut free.

WHEAT- AND GLUTEN-FREE

Sugar Biscuits

Ingredients

150g (5oz) unsalted butter

150g (5oz) caster sugar

1 medium egg

A few drops of vanilla extract

150g (5oz) maize flour

150g (5oz) gluten-free plain flour

1tsp gluten-free baking powder

Makes 22 large or 50 small cookies

TOP TIP

Bake equal-sized biscuits together on a tray so that they take the same amount of time to cook.

1 Preheat the oven to 180°C/350°F/gas mark 4.

2 Line a baking tray with baking parchment.

3 Cream together the butter and caster sugar using a food mixer with a beater attachment or a hand-held electric mixer.

4 Lightly beat the egg then add it into the mixture, along with the vanilla extract.

5 Sieve the flours and baking powder into the mixture and stir to combine them until the mixture forms a dough.

6 Dust the worktop with gluten-free flour and roll out the dough to 5mm (¼") thick.

7 Use cookie cutters to cut out the biscuits and carefully place them on the baking tray with a palette knife or pastry scraper.

8 Bring the leftover dough together and roll out again. Cut out more biscuits until all of the dough is used.

9 Place the tray in the oven and bake for approximately 8 minutes for small biscuits and 13 minutes for larger biscuits. The biscuits should not colour.

10 Decorate as required. For decoration ideas see Animal Sugar Biscuits on page 110.

Variations

To make this recipe dairy free, use dairy-free margarine in place of butter. To make this recipe nut free, ensure the margarine is nut free.

Lemon biscuits: finely grate the zest of 2 lemons into the mixture.

Spicy biscuits: add 3tsp mixed spice or cinnamon with the flour.

Chocolate biscuits: substitute 75g (3oz) maize flour for cocoa powder.

VEGAN, EGG- AND DAIRY-FREE CAKES

Here are my tips for best results:

A vegan sponge cake will be at its best for approximately five days. The vegan and gluten-free version will keep for two to three days. If intended for a celebration cake which needs to be prepared earlier to allow time for decorating, I would suggest using a polystyrene dummy for this tier and making a cutting cake as close to serving as possible.

I use vinegar – either white wine or cider vinegar – in vegan cakes as the acid in the vinegar reacts with the baking powder to make the cakes rise.

As these cakes are crumblier than others, use a sharp serrated knife to carefully saw through and avoid pushing the knife into the cake too hard. A professional bread knife is a good investment. Use a flat baking tray to help move the layers of cooked sponge and save them from breaking.

When portioning the cake, use a knife which has been dipped into boiled water to cut neat slices. Wipe the blade on a piece of clean kitchen paper between each cut.

If you need to dowel your special-diet cake I recommend using thick, hollow American-style dowels such as those made by Wilton as these cakes are softer than other cakes and need extra support (see Suppliers on page 168).

Most of these recipes don't contain nuts but remember to check the ingredient packaging before use to make sure that the products you are using are suitable.

VEGAN, EGG- AND DAIRY-FREE
Vanilla Sponge Cake

Ingredients

510g (1lb 2oz) self-raising flour

335g (11¾oz) caster sugar

A pinch of salt

1tsp baking powder

150ml (5fl oz) sunflower oil

5tsp vinegar (white wine or cider)

510ml (18fl oz) soya milk or 420ml (14¾fl oz) water

A few drops of vanilla extract

Filling

For dairy-free vanilla buttercream, see Cake Fillings, page 88

Makes a 20cm (8") round cake or 27 large cupcakes

This recipe should be nut free, but always check that all of the ingredients are nut free.

1 Line two 20cm (8") round cake tins with silicone-coated parchment paper (see page 28).

2 Preheat the oven to 180°C/350°F/gas mark 4.

3 Mix all of the dry ingredients together in a large bowl.

4 Measure together the wet ingredients, then stir into the dry ingredients. The mixture should be the consistency of a smooth, loose batter.

5 Divide the mixture equally between the cake tins and bake for about 30 minutes until firm to the touch or a knife inserted into the centre comes out clean. Leave to cool for 15 minutes in the tins before turning out first onto a plate then onto a cooling rack so it cools the right way up and doesn't break in half.

Variations

To make this recipe wheat and gluten free, substitute the self-raising flour and baking powder for Doves Farm self-raising gluten-free flour and gluten-free baking powder. You will need to add a little more water until it is the consistency of a smooth, loose batter.

TOP TIPS

When making vegan cupcakes I always use muffin cases, but if you want to use small cupcake cases then divide this mixture in half and reduce the baking time. The cakes should rise to just below the top of the cake cases. Cupcakes are at their best only for a day or two.

Using soya milk gives the sponge more flavour but makes it rather dense. For a lighter sponge, use water instead.

Quantities for a vegan vanilla sponge cake

ROUND AND SQUARE	15cm (6")	20cm (8")	23cm (9")	25cm (10")	30cm (12")
Self-raising flour	350g (12oz)	510g (1lb 2oz)	595g (1lb 5oz)	680g (1lb 8oz)	1.35kg (3lb)
Caster sugar	225g (8oz)	335g (11¾oz)	395g (14oz)	450g (1lb)	900g (2lb)
Salt	½tsp	¾tsp	¾tsp	1tsp	2tsp
Baking powder	1tsp	1½tsp	1¾tsp	2tsp	4tsp
Sunflower oil	100ml (3½fl oz)	150ml (5fl oz)	175ml (6fl oz)	200ml (7fl oz)	400ml (14fl oz)
White wine/cider vinegar	15ml (½fl oz)	23ml (¾fl oz)	26ml (¾fl oz)	30ml (1¼fl oz)	60ml (2¼fl oz)
Cold water	280ml (10fl oz)	420ml (14¾fl oz)	490ml (17¼fl oz)	560ml (19¾fl oz)	1.12l (2 pints)
Divide into 2 tins and bake at 180°C/350°F/gas mark 4.	30 minutes	30 minutes	30 minutes	40–45 minutes	50 minutes–1 hour

VEGAN, EGG- AND DAIRY-FREE
Lemon Cake

Ingredients

510g (1lb 2oz) self-raising flour

335g (11¾oz) caster sugar

A large pinch of salt

1½tsp baking powder

150ml (5fl oz) sunflower oil

5tsp vinegar (white wine or cider)

420ml (14¾fl oz) water

Zest of 2 lemons

For the syrup:

150g (5oz) caster sugar

Juice of 2 lemons

Filling

For dairy-free lemon buttercream, see Cake Fillings (page 88)

Makes a 20cm (8") round cake

This recipe should be nut free, but always check that all of the ingredients are nut free.

1 Line two 20cm (8") round cake tins with silicone-coated parchment paper (see page 28).

2 Preheat the oven to 180°C/350°F/gas mark 4.

3 Mix all of the dry ingredients together in a large bowl.

4 Measure together the wet ingredients, then stir into the dry ingredients. The mixture should be the consistency of a smooth, loose batter.

5 Grate the zest from both lemons into the batter.

6 Divide the mixture equally between the cake tins and bake for about 30 minutes until firm to the touch or a knife inserted into the centre comes out clean. Leave to cool for 15 minutes in the tin before leaving on a cooling rack.

7 When the sponge has cooled, place the juice of the lemons and the remaining 150g (5oz) caster sugar into a saucepan and bring to the boil, stirring constantly. When the sugar has dissolved, split the sponges in half and use a pastry brush to brush each sponge with the lemon syrup.

Variations

To make this recipe wheat and gluten free, substitute the self-raising flour and baking powder for Doves Farm self-raising gluten-free flour and gluten-free baking powder. You will need to add a little more water until it is the consistency of a smooth, loose batter.

VEGAN, EGG- AND DAIRY-FREE
Chocolate Cake

Ingredients

420g (14¾oz) self-raising flour

90g (3¼oz) cocoa powder

1½tsp baking powder

Large pinch of salt

335g (12oz) caster sugar

150ml (5fl oz) sunflower oil

5tsp vinegar (white wine or cider)

600ml (21fl oz) water

A few drops of vanilla extract

75g (3oz) dairy-free plain chocolate

150g (5oz) dairy-free chocolate chips

Filling

For dairy-free chocolate ganache, see
Cake Fillings, page 84

Makes a 20cm (8") round cake

1 Line two 20cm (8") round cake tins with silicone-coated parchment paper (see page 28).

2 Preheat the oven to 180°C/350°F/gas mark 4.

3 Sieve together the flour, cocoa powder, baking powder and salt into a large bowl. Stir in the sugar.

4 Measure together the sunflower oil, vinegar, water and vanilla extract and stir this into the dry ingredients. The mixture should be the consistency of a smooth, loose batter.

5 Melt the chocolate in the microwave on low, stirring every 30 seconds until melted, or in a bowl over a pan of just-boiled water (making sure the base of the bowl does not come into contact with the water or the chocolate may 'seize'). Stir the melted chocolate into the batter.

6 Stir in the chocolate chips.

7 Divide the mixture equally between the cake tins and bake for about 30 minutes until firm to the touch or a knife inserted comes out clean. Leave to cool for 15 minutes in the tin before leaving on a cooling rack.

Variations

To make this recipe wheat and gluten free, substitute the self-raising flour and baking powder for Doves Farm self-raising gluten-free flour, gluten-free cocoa powder and gluten-free baking powder. You will need to add a little more water until it is the consistency of a smooth, loose batter.

To make this recipe nut free, ensure the chocolate, cocoa powder and chocolate chips are nut free.

VEGAN, EGG- AND DAIRY-FREE
Carrot Cake

Ingredients

510g (1lb 2oz) self-raising flour

335g (11¾oz) demerara sugar

A large pinch of salt

1½tsp baking powder

4tsp mixed spice

150ml (5fl oz) sunflower oil

5tsp vinegar (white wine or cider)

420ml (14¾fl oz) water

A few drops of vanilla extract

150g (5oz) carrots, grated

90g (3¼oz) raisins

Filling

For dairy-free orange buttercream, see
Cake Fillings, page 87

Makes a 20cm (8") round cake

This recipe should be nut free,
but always check that all of the
ingredients are nut free.

1 Line two 20cm (8") round cake tins
with silicone-coated parchment paper
(see page 28).

2 Preheat the oven to 180°C/350°F/gas
mark 4.

3 Mix all of the dry ingredients together
in a large bowl.

4 Measure together the wet ingredients,
then stir these into the dry ingredients.

5 Stir in the grated carrots and raisins.
The mixture should be the consistency
of a smooth, loose batter.

6 Divide the mixture equally between
the tins and bake for about 30 minutes
until firm to the touch or a knife inserted
into the centre comes out clean. Leave
to cool for 15 minutes in the tin before
leaving on a cooling rack.

Variations

To make this recipe wheat and gluten free, substitute the self-raising flour and
baking powder for Doves Farm self-raising gluten-free flour and gluten-free baking
powder. You will need to add a little more water until it is the consistency of a
smooth, loose batter.

VEGAN, EGG- AND DAIRY-FREE
Fruit Cake

Ingredients

450g (1lb) sultanas

110g (4oz) raisins

110g (4oz) currants

90g (3¼oz) mixed peel

90g (3¼oz) glacé cherries

75ml (3fl oz) vegan brandy

510g (1lb 2oz) self-raising flour

335g (11¾oz) soft dark brown sugar

A large pinch of salt

1½tsp baking powder

2tsp mixed spice

1tsp ground nutmeg

150ml (5fl oz) sunflower oil

5tsp vinegar (white wine or cider)

450ml (15¾fl oz) water

Makes a 20cm (8") round cake

This recipe should be nut free, but always check that all of the ingredients are nut free.

1 Place the sultanas, raisins, currants, mixed peel, cherries and brandy in a large bowl, cover and leave to soak overnight.

2 Line a 20cm (8") cake tin with silicone-coated parchment paper (see page 28).

3 Preheat the oven to 160°C/325°F/gas mark 3.

4 Mix all of the dry ingredients together in a large bowl.

5 Measure together the wet ingredients then stir into the dry ingredients. The mixture should be the consistency of a smooth, loose batter.

6 Stir in the soaked dried fruit.

7 Pour into the cake tin, then cover the cake tin with a piece of tin foil with a hole in the middle. Cut a piece of greaseproof paper big enough to wrap around the cake tin twice. Fold over lengthways three or four times to the same height as the cake tin. Wrap this around the cake tin and secure with sticky tape.

8 Bake for about 3½–4 hours or until a knife inserted into the centre comes out clean. Leave to cool in the cake tin to help keep its shape.

Please note this fruit cake will only keep for about five days.

Variations

To make this recipe wheat and gluten free, substitute the self-raising flour and baking powder for Doves Farm self-raising gluten-free flour and gluten-free baking powder. You will need to add a little more water until it is the consistency of a smooth, loose batter.

Ensure the dried fruit, mixed peel and glacé cherries are wheat free.

This cake will keep for four or five days.

Quantities for a vegan fruit cake

ROUND	15cm (6")	20cm (8")	23cm (9")	25cm (10")	30cm (12")
SQUARE	13cm (5")	18cm (7")	20cm (8")	23cm (9")	30cm (12")
Currants	75g (3oz)	110g (4oz)	150g (5oz)	180g (3¼oz)	360g (12oz)
Raisins	75g (3oz)	110g (4oz)	150g (5oz)	180g (3¼oz)	360g (12oz)
Sultanas	300g (10oz)	450g (1lb)	600g (1lb 5½oz)	750g (1lb 10½oz)	1.5kg (3lb 5oz)
Mixed peel	60g (2¼oz)	90g (3¼oz)	120g (4oz)	150g (5oz)	300g (10oz)
Glacé cherries	60g (2¼oz)	90g (3¼oz)	120g (4oz)	150g (5oz)	300g (10oz)
Vegan brandy	50ml (2fl oz)	75ml (3fl oz)	100ml (3½fl oz)	125ml (4fl oz)	250ml (9fl oz)
Self-raising flour	225g (8oz)	510g (1lb 2oz)	510g (1lb 2oz)	595g (1lb 5oz)	1190g (2lb 10oz)
Dark brown sugar	170g (6oz)	335g (12oz)	340g (12oz)	390g (13¾oz)	780g (1lb 11½oz)
Salt	½tsp	¾tsp	¾tsp	¾tsp	1½tsp
Baking powder	¾tsp	1½tsp	1½tsp	1¾tsp	3½tsp
Mixed spice	1tsp	2tsp	2tsp	2½tsp	5tsp
Nutmeg	½tsp	1tsp	1tsp	1¼tsp	2½tsp
Sunflower oil	75ml (3fl oz)	150ml (5fl oz)	150-ml (5fl oz)	175ml (6fl oz)	350ml (12fl oz)
White wine/ cider vinegar	12ml (½fl oz)	23ml (¾fl oz)	23ml (¾fl oz)	26ml (1fl oz)	52ml (2fl oz)
Cold water	225ml (8fl oz)	450ml (15¾fl oz)	450ml (15¾fl oz)	525ml (18½fl oz)	1.2l (2 pints)
Bake at 160°C/325°F/gas mark 3.	2–3 hours	3½–4 hours	3½–4 hours	4–4½ hours	4–5 hours

VEGAN, EGG- AND DAIRY-FREE
Coffee and Walnut Cake

Ingredients

435g (15¼oz) self-raising flour

335g (11¾oz) demerara sugar

A large pinch of salt

1½tsp baking powder

75g (3oz) ground walnuts

4tsp instant coffee granules

420ml (14¾fl oz) water

150ml (5¼fl oz) sunflower oil

5tsp vinegar (white wine or cider)

A few drops of vanilla extract

75g (3oz) walnuts, roughly chopped

Filling

For dairy-free coffee buttercream, see Cake Fillings, page 87

Makes a 20cm (8") round cake

1 Line two 20cm (8") round cake tins with silicone-coated parchment paper (see page 28).

2 Preheat the oven to 180°C/350°F/gas mark 4.

3 Mix the flour, sugar, salt, baking powder and ground walnuts together in a large bowl.

4 Dissolve the coffee in a little boiling water then top up with cold water to 420ml (14¾fl oz). Add the sunflower oil, white wine/cider vinegar and vanilla extract and stir into the dry ingredients. The mixture should be the consistency of a smooth, loose batter. Stir in the chopped walnuts.

5 Divide the mixture equally between the cake tins and bake for about 30 minutes until firm to the touch or a knife inserted into the centre comes out clean.

6 Leave to cool for 15 minutes in the tin before leaving on a cooling rack.

Variations

To make this recipe wheat and gluten free, substitute the self-raising flour and baking powder for Doves Farm self-raising gluten-free flour and gluten-free baking powder. You will need to add a little more water until it is the consistency of a smooth, loose batter.

To make this recipe nut free, omit the ground and chopped walnuts from the recipe.

VEGAN, EGG- AND DAIRY-FREE
Coconut Cake

Ingredients

50g (2oz) creamed coconut

420ml (14¾fl oz) water

435g (15¼oz) self-raising flour

335g (11¾oz) caster sugar

A pinch of salt

1½tsp baking powder

75g (3oz) desiccated coconut

150ml (5fl oz) sunflower oil

5tsp vinegar (white wine or cider)

Filling

For dairy-free vanilla buttercream, see Cake Fillings, page 88

Makes a 20cm (8") round cake

1 Line two 20cm (8") round cake tins with silicone-coated parchment paper (see page 28).

2 Preheat the oven to 180°C/350°F/gas mark 4.

3 Place the creamed coconut in a bowl and pour over enough boiling water to melt the coconut from the total amount of water in the recipe. When melted, top up with the rest of the cold water.

4 Mix all of the dry ingredients together in a large bowl.

5 Measure together the wet ingredients then stir these into the dry ingredients. The mixture should be the consistency of a smooth, loose batter.

6 Stir in the melted creamed coconut.

7 Divide the mixture equally between the cake tins and bake for about 30 minutes until firm to the touch or a knife inserted into the centre comes out clean. Leave to cool for 15 minutes in the tin before leaving on a cooling rack.

Variations

To make this recipe wheat and gluten free, substitute the self-raising flour and baking powder for Doves Farm self-raising gluten-free flour and gluten-free baking powder. You will need to add a little more water until it is the consistency of a smooth, loose batter.

To make this recipe nut free, see note on page 58 regarding the use of coconut in nut-free cakes.

VEGAN, EGG- AND DAIRY-FREE

Shortbread

Ingredients

70g (2½oz) caster sugar

140g (4¾oz) dairy-free margarine

200g (7oz) plain flour

Makes 12 x 7.5cm (3") round biscuits

1 Preheat the oven to 180°C/350°F/gas mark 4.

2 Cream the sugar with the dairy-free margarine until light and fluffy.

3 Mix in the flour and bring together to form a dough.

4 Roll out to a 5mm (¼") thickness and press out shapes using biscuit cutters.

5 Place onto a baking tray lined with greaseproof paper brushed with oil or silicone-coated baking parchment.

6 Bake small biscuits for 8 minutes and larger biscuits for 13–15 minutes. Leave on the baking tray to cool. Always bake similar-sized biscuits together so they cook at the same time.

7 Decorate as required. For decoration ideas see Animal Sugar Biscuits or Shortbread on page 110.

Variations

To make this recipe gluten free, use 100g (3½oz) maize flour or cornflour and 100g (3½oz) gluten-free plain flour in place of the plain flour.

To make this recipe nut free, ensure the margarine is nut free.

VEGAN, EGG- AND DAIRY-FREE

Ingredients

100g (3½oz) dairy-free margarine

75g (3oz) soft dark brown sugar

50g (2oz) golden syrup

200g (7oz) self-raising flour

1tsp mixed spice

2tsp ground ginger

Makes 14–16 biscuits

Variations

To make this recipe gluten free, see the gluten-free gingerbread recipe on page 63.

To make this recipe nut free, ensure the margarine is nut free.

1 Line a baking tray with greaseproof paper or silicone-coated baking parchment (see page 28).

2 Preheat the oven to 180°C/350°F/gas mark 4.

3 In a saucepan melt together the dairy-free margarine, soft dark brown sugar and golden syrup. Leave to cool slightly.

4 Sieve together the self-raising flour, mixed spice and ground ginger. Stir into the melted ingredients to form a dough. If it looks too runny leave it to cool before rolling out.

5 Roll out the dough to a 5mm (¼") thickness. Cut out the biscuits using a cookie cutter.

6 Bake small biscuits for 8 minutes and larger biscuits for 13–15 minutes. Leave on the baking tray to cool. Always bake similar-sized biscuits together so they are equally cooked.

7 Decorate as required. For decoration ideas, see Christmas Gingerbread on page 113.

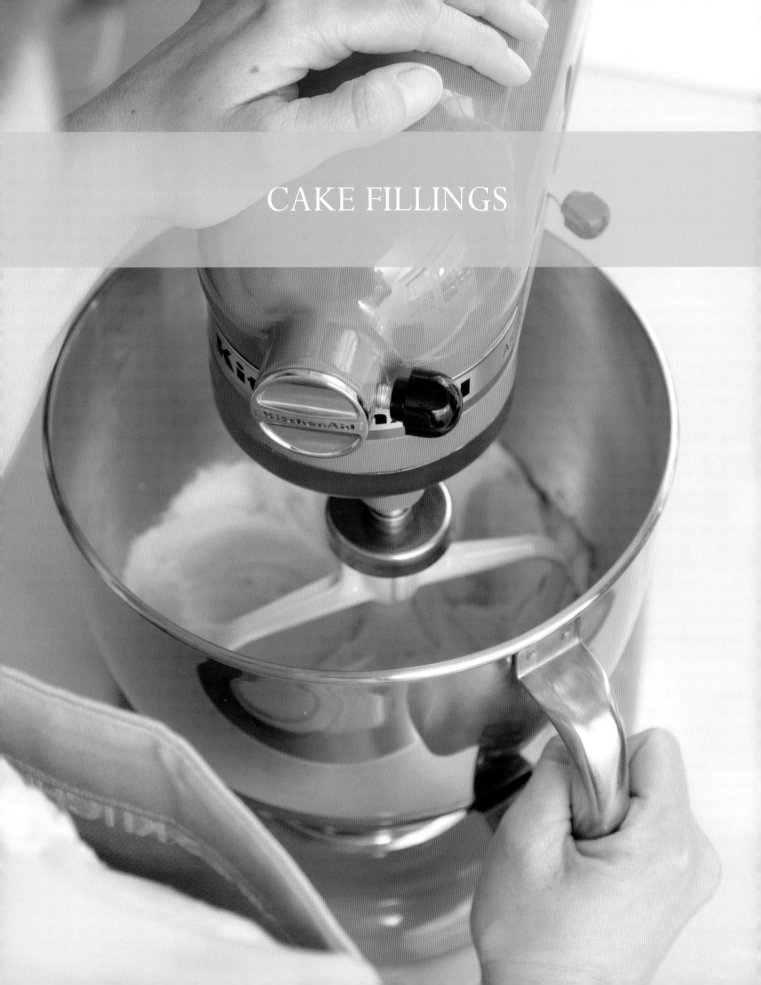

CAKE FILLINGS

Chocolate Ganache

Ingredients

150g (5oz) plain couverture chocolate (55–60% cocoa solids)

150g (5oz) milk couverture chocolate

200ml (7fl oz) double cream

1 Chop the chocolate into small chunks.

2 Place the cream into a saucepan and bring to the boil.

3 Turn off the heat and stir in the chocolate until melted.

4 Use for covering and filling a chocolate cake or for piping.

Covering a cake with ganache (pouring method)

1 While the ganache is still warm, place a prepared and filled cake on a plate or cake board of the same size. I usually coat the cake with chocolate paste first to give a smooth base over which to pour the ganache. Place a cooling rack over a large, clean baking tray.

2 Allow the ganache to cool to 32°C/90°F. Place the cake on the cooling rack and pour the warm ganache over the top, making sure the cake is completely covered.

3 Leave the ganache to pour off the cake onto the tray. When it has set on the cake, the leftover ganache from the tray can be used again to cover and fill cakes.

TOP TIP Do not reuse the leftover ganache for other special diet cakes as it may contain cake crumbs.

4 Keep any leftover ganache in an airtight container in the fridge for up to four weeks or use to make truffles.

Variations

To make white chocolate ganache, replace the milk and plain chocolate in the recipe with white chocolate. It will not set as firm as if you were using milk or plain chocolate. The colour of white chocolate ganache is opaque and a little yellow in colour. To make a whiter ganache, lightly whisk it and apply to the cake quickly before it sets. Be careful not to whisk it too much or it will split.

Liqueurs or flavourings can be added to the melted ganache mixture. Check that the ingredients of the liqueurs are suitable for your special diet.

To make this recipe nut free, ensure the chocolate is nut free.

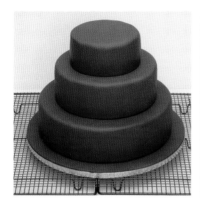

The following quantities are sufficient to fill and crumb-coat a cake when a thin coat is required prior to covering with sugarpaste or chocolate paste (see page 98). For covering a cake with a thicker layer of ganache, you will need to increase these amounts.

Quantities to fill and crumb-coat a cake with ganache

ROUND OR SQUARE	15cm (6")	20cm (8")	23cm (9")	25cm (10")	30cm (12")
Plain chocolate	110g (4oz)	150g (5oz)	225g (8oz)	300g (10oz)	450g (1lb)
Milk chocolate	110g (4oz)	150g (5oz)	225g (8oz)	300g (10oz)	450g (1lb)
Double cream	150ml (5fl oz)	200ml (7fl oz)	300ml (10fl oz)	400ml (14½fl oz)	600ml (1 pint)

TOP TIPS

For filling a cake, leave the ganache to cool and set overnight at room temperature before filling and spreading over the cake, otherwise it will be too runny.

For a lighter ganache, place in a mixing bowl and beat for a few seconds until it turns lighter in colour; this incorporates air which makes it quite mousse-like. Use this straight away as it becomes firm if left to stand. Use to fill and spread all over the cake, leaving a rough pattern.

Once whisked, use ganache containing dairy cream straight away or it will harden and become difficult to smooth over the sponge. In order to use the ganache over a longer period of time, do not whisk it before spreading.

Whisked ganache can also be piped. Fit a star-shaped nozzle into a large piping bag, fill the bag with ganache and pipe around the bottom of the cake.

Dairy-free ganache cannot be whisked.

I prefer to use half plain and half milk chocolate in ganache as I feel using only milk chocolate is too sweet and only plain chocolate too rich.

It is important to use plain chocolate containing 55–60% cocoa solids in ganache. A higher cocoa content will produce a ganache which is too firm.

To make simple but delicious truffles with leftover ganache, pipe small balls onto a piece of greaseproof paper. Leave to set in the fridge and then coat in melted chocolate, toasted chopped nuts or cocoa powder.

DAIRY-FREE
Chocolate Ganache

Ingredients

200ml (7fl oz) almond milk

300g (10oz) dairy-free plain chocolate, broken into chunks (55–60% cocoa solids; do not use chocolate with a higher cocoa solid content as it will make the ganache too firm when set)

Variations

To make this recipe nut free, ganache can be made using soya milk in the same way but will need to be kept in the fridge and consumed within five days or it will go mouldy. The ganache can also be made using coconut milk (see note on page 58 regarding the use of coconut in nut-free cakes), although this does give it quite a strong flavour. Ensure the chocolate is nut free.

1 Bring the milk to the boil. Take off the heat and stir in the chocolate until melted and smooth.

2 Allow the ganache to cool to 32°C/90°F. Pour over a prepared cake to achieve a smooth finish (see instructions for the Chocolate Gerbera Cake on page 127) or leave to set overnight at room temperature before using to fill a cake.

TOP TIPS

This recipe for ganache is not suitable for crumb-coating a cake if it is also to be covered with sugarpaste, marzipan or chocolate paste as it is too wet and the icing will slide off. Instead, use dairy-free buttercream for crumb-coating (see recipe on page 88).

For a lighter chocolate ganache, try mixing the ganache with an equal quantity of dairy-free buttercream or use 150g (5oz) each of dairy-free plain and milk chocolate instead of 300g (10oz) dairy-free plain chocolate. Dairy-free ganache cannot be whisked.

Both dairy-free ganache recipes can be used for piping. Use large Savoy piping nozzles and a nylon piping bag.

To make really good dairy-free chocolate truffles, melt together equal quantities of 73% dairy-free plain chocolate and almond milk. Add any flavourings or liqueurs, leave to set and roll into truffles.

DAIRY-FREE

White Chocolate Ganache

Ingredients

400g (14oz) dairy-free white chocolate, broken into chunks

200ml (7oz) almond milk

1 Bring the milk to the boil.

2 Take off the heat and stir in the chocolate pieces until melted.

3 Leave to set before using.

TOP TIP Not all dairy-free white chocolate will work for this recipe. However, I have found that Humdinger Dairy Free White Buttons work really well.

Variations

To make this recipe nut free, ganache can be made using soya milk in the same way but will need to be kept in the fridge and consumed within five days or it will go mouldy. The ganache can also be made using coconut milk (see note on page 58 regarding the use of coconut in nut-free cakes), although this does give it quite a strong flavour. Ensure the chocolate is nut free.

Quantities to fill a cake with dairy-free chocolate ganache

ROUND OR SQUARE	15cm (6")	20cm (8")	23cm (9")	25cm (10")	30cm (12")
Dairy-free plain chocolate (55–60% cocoa solids)	225g (8oz)	300g (10oz)	450g (1lb)	600g (1lb 5¼oz)	900g (2lb)
Almond milk	150ml (5fl oz)	200ml (7fl oz)	300ml (10fl oz)	400ml (14fl oz)	600ml (1 pint)

Buttercream

Ingredients

250g (9oz) unsalted butter at room temperature

500g (1lb 1oz) icing sugar

1 Beat the butter to soften it using a food mixer or a hand-held electric mixer.

2 Add the icing sugar and mix into the butter slowly.

3 Add the flavouring of your choice.

4 Once the icing sugar is mixed into the butter, increase the speed and beat until light and fluffy. Add a few drops of water if the buttercream looks too firm.

Variations

Vanilla buttercream: add a few drops of vanilla extract to taste.

Orange buttercream: stir in finely grated orange zest to taste.

Lemon buttercream: stir in finely grated lemon zest to taste.

Coffee buttercream: add 2 dessertspoons of instant coffee granules diluted with a small amount of boiling water.

Quantities to fill and crumb-coat a cake with buttercream

ROUND OR SQUARE	15cm (6")	20cm (8")	23cm (9")	25cm (10")	30cm (12")
Unsalted butter	200g (7oz)	250g (9oz)	300g (10oz)	400g (14oz)	500g (1lb 1oz)
Icing sugar	400g (14oz)	500g (1lb 1oz)	600 (14oz)	800g (1lb 12oz)	1kg (2lb 3oz)

DAIRY-FREE

Buttercream

Ingredients

200g (7oz) dairy-free margarine

800g (1lb 12oz) icing sugar

1 Mix the icing sugar and any flavouring (as for buttercream on page 87) into the dairy-free margarine. Do not over-beat the mixture as it can split.

2 Stir in a few drops of water until it reaches the required consistency.

Variations

To make this recipe nut free, ensure the margarine is nut free.

TOP TIP

It may seem as though there is a lot of icing sugar, but any less will cause the mixture to split. Add a little extra flavouring to this buttercream to make up for the amount of sugar. It is very sweet so you do not need to use as much as you usually would.

Quantities to fill and crumb-coat a cake with dairy-free buttercream

ROUND OR SQUARE	15cm (6")	20cm (8")	23cm (9")	25cm (10")	30cm (12")
Dairy-free margarine	150g (5oz)	200g (7oz)	250g (9oz)	300g (10oz)	400g (14oz)
Icing sugar	600g (1lb 5¼oz)	800g (1lb 12oz)	1kg (2lb 3¼oz)	1.2kg (2lb 10¼oz)	1.6kg (3lb 8½oz)

American Frosting

Ingredients

500g (1lb 1oz) icing sugar

125g (4oz) white vegetable fat
(e.g. Trex or White Flora)

Vanilla extract (check it is suitable for
the special diet)

Paste food colouring (check the
ingredients are suitable, see table on
page 159)

1 Using a food mixer, mix the icing
sugar into the white fat slowly until
combined. Add a few drops of vanilla
extract.

2 Continue mixing a little faster for 5
minutes.

3 Add colouring to the frosting if
required.

4 Mix 75ml (5tbsp) of cold water to
the frosting before using for piping or
coating a cake.

TOP TIP

American frosting is
a good alternative to
dairy-free buttercream for
decorating as it is pure
white and may also be
coloured. It can be used
to coat a cake and to pipe
scrolls and other designs,
including flowers, instead
of using royal icing. Once
set, it is hard enough to be
handled.

WHEAT- AND GLUTEN-FREE

Pastry Cream (Crème Patissière)

Ingredients

280ml (10fl oz) milk

50g (2oz) caster sugar

2 medium eggs

40g (1½oz) cornflour

2tsp gluten-free custard powder

A few drops of vanilla extract

Make sure you stir the custard over a low heat. If the heat is too high, the mixture will scramble.

1 Pour the milk into a large saucepan and place on the heat.

2 Beat the sugar and eggs together until white and creamy. Stir the cornflour and custard powder into the egg. Add the vanilla extract.

3 When the milk has come to the boil, whisk half the milk into the egg mixture then pour this back into the hot milk. Stir over a low heat until the mixture thickens then beat until smooth.

4 Pour through a sieve into a clean bowl. Cool and store in a fridge until needed.

Variations

To make this recipe dairy free, use your choice of dairy-free milk in place of cow's milk. I prefer to use almond milk.

To make chocolate pastry cream, stir in 50g (2oz) gluten- and dairy-free cocoa powder with the cornflour and custard powder. For a richer chocolate pastry cream, stir 50g (2oz) melted gluten- and dairy-free plain chocolate into the cooked pastry cream while still hot.

For a rich pastry cream, fold 150g (5oz) whipped cream into the cold pastry cream.

VEGAN AND GLUTEN-FREE MODELLING PASTES

VEGAN AND GLUTEN-FREE

Sugarpaste

Sugarpaste suitable for vegans, nut-, wheat- and gluten-free diets is easily available (see page 156) and reliable but if you want to try making it yourself, why not give this recipe a go?

Ingredients

550g (1lb 3oz) icing sugar

2tsp gum tragacanth

2tsp Dr Oetker Vege-Gel

4tsp glucose syrup

2tsp glycerine

2tsp white vegetable fat

A few drops of vanilla extract

This recipe should be nut free, but always check that all of the ingredients are nut free.

1 Place the icing sugar in a large bowl or food mixer bowl. Stir in the gum tragacanth.

2 Stir the Vege-Gel with 65ml (2fl oz) cold water until dissolved. Heat the mixture to boiling point.

3 Mix the rest of the ingredients into the Vege-Gel until melted. Stir this into the icing sugar.

4 When the mixture becomes too stiff to mix, pour onto the table and knead until smooth. If using a food mixer, mix until smooth. The icing will be quite soft.

5 Place in a freezer bag and then into a sealed container and leave to rest for at least a day before using.

VEGAN AND GLUTEN-FREE

Mexican Paste

This can be used to make models. If you need a stronger modelling paste, for example for making frills around a cake, draped fabric effect or bows, mix equal amounts of flower paste and sugarpaste together and use straight away.

Ingredients

1tsp gum tragacanth

250g (9oz) sugarpaste (shop-bought or homemade), nut-free if needed

1 Knead the gum tragacanth into the sugarpaste.

2 Place in a freezer bag, expel the air and seal. Leave until the next day to use.

VEGAN AND GLUTEN-FREE

Flower Paste

NUT-FREE

'Marzipan'

Ready-made flower paste suitable for these diets is available (see page 157). For anyone who usually makes their own gelatine-based flower paste and needs a vegan alternative, this recipe is easy to make and works really well. Flower paste is used to make delicate sugar flowers and models for cakes as it can be rolled out quite finely. It does dry quickly, so work with small pieces at a time and keep the rest of the paste sealed in a freezer bag in a plastic container. This paste dries very hard.

This recipe is from Kathy Moore's first book Cakes from Concept to Creation (B. Dutton Publishing) and is a great alternative to marzipan. Always check the ingredients to make sure they are suitable for a nut-free diet.

Ingredients

500g (1lb 1oz) icing sugar

40ml (1½fl oz) gum tragacanth

2tsp Vege-Gel

4tsp white vegetable fat

2tsp wheat-free glucose syrup

A few drops of vanilla extract

This recipe should be nut free, but always check that all of the ingredients are nut free.

1 Place the icing sugar in a large bowl or food mixer bowl. Stir in the gum tragacanth.

2 Stir the Vege-Gel with 85ml (3fl oz) water until dissolved. Heat the mixture to boiling point.

3 Mix the rest of the ingredients into the Vege-Gel until melted. Stir this into the icing sugar. If the mixture is too dry add a further 2tsp water. When the mixture becomes too stiff to mix, pour onto the table and knead until smooth. If using a food mixer, mix until smooth. The icing will be quite soft.

4 Place into a freezer bag, expel the air and seal. Place into an airtight container and leave for at least a day to rest before using. Store in the fridge for up to two weeks.

Ingredients

100g (3½oz) semolina

50g (1¾oz) margarine

Nut-free almond essence, to taste

2tbsp pre-boiled water

100g (3½oz) granulated sugar

CONTAINS WHEAT AND GLUTEN.

1 Place the margarine and the water in a saucepan and melt over a gentle heat.

2 Add the semolina and stir for a minute.

3 Stir in the sugar, then add the flavouring.

4 Cool until stiff and knead very lightly to bring all the ingredients together. Leave until cold before use.

5 To cover cakes, knead in a little icing sugar and roll out onto a non-stick board dusted with icing sugar. For a stiffer paste, slightly increase the quantity of semolina.

VEGAN AND GLUTEN-FREE
Pastillage

Pastillage can be rolled out quite thinly and shapes can be cut from it to make large flat pieces of sugar decoration. For example, you would use pastillage for walls for sugar replica buildings or a plaque which needs to dry hard and be strong enough to stand up without support. Pastillage dries very hard so make sure the recipient knows this before the cake is served.

Ingredients

500g (1lb 1oz) icing sugar

30ml (2tbsp) cornflour

3g (½tsp) gum tragacanth

10g (2tsp) Vege-Gel

This recipe should be nut free, but always check that all of the ingredients are nut free.

1 Sieve the icing sugar, cornflour and gum tragacanth into a large bowl.

2 Stir the Vege-Gel with 60g (2¼fl oz) water until dissolved. Heat the mixture to boiling point.

3 Mix the Vege-Gel into the icing sugar mixture. When it is too stiff to mix, turn out onto the table and knead until smooth.

4 Place into a freezer bag, expel the air and seal. Place into an airtight container and leave for a day before using. Store in the fridge for up to two weeks.

TOP TIP

This recipe takes a little longer to dry than regular pastillage. Allow three or four days' extra drying time for large or thick pieces. Leave cut-out pieces of pastillage on a wooden chopping board or a piece of cardboard to dry. This helps the underneath of the piece to dry and prevents warping.

To avoid dragging the pastillage out of shape, cut from one edge towards the centre, then the other edge towards the centre.

VEGAN AND GLUTEN-FREE
Chocolate Modelling Paste

This paste can be used for covering cakes as well as modelling.

Ingredients

180g (6½oz) wheat-free and dairy-free plain couverture chocolate (55–60% cocoa solids. You can use a higher cocoa content but this will make a firmer modelling paste)

140g (4¾oz) glucose syrup (see list on page 160)

300g (10oz) sugarpaste (shop-bought or homemade)

1 Melt the chocolate in a microwave on low, stirring every 30 seconds until melted, or in a bowl set over a pan of just boiled water (make sure the base of the bowl doesn't come into contact with the water or the chocolate may 'seize').

2 Warm the glucose syrup for a few seconds in a microwave.

3 Mix the two together. The mixture will thicken to a paste.

4 Knead this mixture with the sugarpaste until combined. Small amounts can be mixed together in a food mixer.

5 Seal in a freezer bag, expelling all air, and leave for a day to rest before using.

Variations

For a white chocolate version, use 250g (9oz) vegan white chocolate, 140g (4¾oz) glucose syrup and 400g (14oz) sugarpaste and make in the same way.

To make this recipe nut free, ensure the chocolate and sugarpaste are nut free.

Preparing Cakes for Decorating

When you are preparing special-diet cakes for decorating, there are a few extra considerations that are worth remembering to make sure you don't introduce allergens through cross-contamination:

Prepare, bake, fill and cover special-diet cakes at different times to other cakes to prevent cross-contamination.

Labelling your utensils is a good idea: I have one nylon piping bag which I only use for dairy-free fillings to prevent cross-contamination.

If you make a lot of cakes for special diets, always label leftover sugarpaste, marzipan and chocolate paste with what type of cake it was used for, or use a fresh batch for special-diet cakes.

See the food labelling section starting on page 14 for details on how food labelling regulations require you to label cakes made for sale, particularly those for special diets.

As these cakes are crumblier than others, use a sharp, serrated knife to carefully saw through and avoid pushing the knife into the cake too hard. A professional bread knife is a good investment.

PREPARING A SPECIAL-DIET SPONGE CAKE FOR COVERING WITH SUGARPASTE OR CHOCOLATE PASTE (CRUMB-COAT)

You will need:

Special-diet sponge cake or chocolate cake

Jam

Dairy/dairy-free buttercream or chocolate ganache/nut-free ganache (see pages 87, 88 and 82)

Thin, heavy-duty cake board the same size as the cake

Large bread knife

Small palette knife

Straight edged plastic pastry scraper

1 Ensure all equipment and work surfaces are clean. Do not prepare special-diet cakes at the same time as other cakes.

2 Carve the very top off each sponge cake with a large bread knife. Turn the cake upside down to check the cake is level: if not, turn it the other way up again and carve away a little more cake to make it level.

3 Once level, turn both sponges upside down. Cut each sponge in half horizontally and line up the layers on your worktop.

4 Using a small palette knife, spread a little buttercream or chocolate ganache onto the cake board. Sit the first layer of sponge on top and spread this with a thin layer of jam then buttercream or chocolate ganache.

5 Place the next two layers on top of this, spreading with a thin layer of jam and buttercream or chocolate ganache between each one.

6 Position the last layer on top. Check the top is level and the sides of the cake are straight.

7 Coat the top and sides of the cake with a thin layer of buttercream or ganache to crumb-coat the cake.

8 Use a plastic pastry scraper to scrape off the excess buttercream from the sides and to give a smooth finish; any bumps will show through the icing.

9 If the buttercream or chocolate ganache on the cake is quite soft, place the cake in the fridge for an hour or so to firm before covering with sugarpaste.

TOP TIP

Do not use dairy-free chocolate ganache to crumb-coat the outside of the cake prior to covering with sugarpaste or other covering: the ganache is too wet and the paste will become soggy and slide down the cake. Instead, use dairy-free 'buttercream' to coat the outside of the cake (see recipe on page 88).

COVERING A VEGAN, DAIRY-FREE OR WHEAT- AND GLUTEN-FREE FRUIT CAKE WITH MARZIPAN

You will need:

Fruit cake

Vegan brandy

Marzipan or nut-free 'marzipan' (see recipe on page 93). Make sure to use a fresh batch for every cake

Large bread knife

Icing sugar in a sugar shaker

Heavy-duty cake board, the same size as the cake

Cake drum/board the same shape and at least 7.5cm (3") wider than the cake (depending on your cake design)

Silicone pastry brush

Large rolling pin (if this is also used to roll out pastry, make sure it is scrupulously clean)

Cake smoother

Small knife

Cardboard cake box for storage

1 Carve the very top off the fruit cake with a large bread knife. Turn the cake upside down to check the cake is level. If not turn the other way up again and carve away a little more cake to make it level.

2 When level, brush the carved side with brandy using a clean pastry brush and place it upside down on the cake board.

3 If there is a gap between the bottom edge of the cake and the cake board, roll a long sausage of marzipan and push this into the gap. Trim the marzipan flush with the side of the cake. If there are any large holes in the cake where the fruit has fallen out, fill these with marzipan.

4 Brush the cake with brandy. Do not pour leftover brandy back into the bottle. If there is a lot leftover, cover it and label it with what it has been used for.

5 Quickly knead the marzipan, dust the worktop with icing sugar and roll out the marzipan about 5mm (¼") thick (or thicker if you prefer). Roll it large enough to cover the whole cake.

6 Place the marzipan on top of the cake and smooth the surface to make sure it sticks to the cake and there are no air bubbles.

7 Use your hand to smooth the marzipan onto the side of the cake. If the marzipan creases, pull it away from the cake, straighten the crease and smooth it back down. Run over the marzipan with a cake smoother. If you are covering a square cake, smooth the marzipan to the four corners first then smooth the sides.

8 Leave 2cm (¾") of marzipan around the bottom of the cake and trim away the rest.

9 Sit the cake on top of a smaller bowl or turntable. Run over the cake again with the cake smoother until the marzipan overhangs the cake board. Trim the marzipan at the bottom of the cake flush with the bottom of the cake board. Smooth with your hand to leave a neat finish.

10 Once covered with marzipan, leave a fruit cake to dry for at least for two days but ideally for five days before icing. Store on top of the cake drum in a cardboard cake box. Ice a vegan fruit cake straight away as it will only keep for one week.

COVERING A VEGAN, DAIRY-FREE OR WHEAT- AND GLUTEN-FREE CAKE WITH SUGARPASTE

You will need:

Sponge cake filled and coated with buttercream (see pages 98 to 99) or a fruit cake covered with marzipan (see pages 100 to 101), complete with cake board

Vegan brandy (if covering a fruit cake)

Sugarpaste, see recipe on page 92 (use a fresh batch or sugarpaste which has been used to decorate a cake suitable for the same diet)

Large bread knife

Icing sugar in a sugar shaker

Cake drum/board at least 7.5cm (3") wider than the cake

Silicone pastry brush

Large plastic rolling pin (if this is used to roll out pastry make sure it is scrupulously clean)

Cake smoother

Small sharp knife

Scribing needle, or sterilised glass-headed pin which is kept only for cake use (for popping any air bubbles)

1 Plan how you want to decorate the cake before covering in case you want to use embossers or crimpers or mark out a pattern. Make any templates needed and ensure your equipment and work surfaces are clean.

2 Cover the cake board first. Knead $1/3$ of the sugarpaste until smooth and pliable.

3 Dust the work surface with icing sugar and roll out the sugarpaste so it is big enough to cover the cake board. Move it around the worktop between rolls to stop it sticking.

4 Brush a little pre-boiled water onto the cake board to help the paste stick. Lift the sugarpaste onto the cake board and smooth over. Trim the edge flush with the edge of the cake board.

5 If covering a marzipanned fruit cake, brush the cake with brandy. Do not pour leftover brandy back into the bottle: if there is a lot leftover, cover it and label it with what it has been used for and don't use it for special-diet cakes.

6 Knead the rest of the sugarpaste until smooth and pliable.

7 Dust the worktop with icing sugar. Roll out the sugarpaste wide enough to cover the cake. Move it around the worktop between rolls to prevent it sticking, adding more icing sugar to the worktop if needed. If there are any air bubbles, pierce these with a clean scribing needle.

8 Lift the sugarpaste and place it over the cake.

9 Smooth the sugarpaste onto the top, then onto the sides of the cake. If it creases, lift the paste away from the cake, smooth out and push it back onto the cake. Run over the surface with a cake smoother.

10 Leave 2cm (¾") sugarpaste around the bottom of the cake and trim away the rest.

11 Sit the cake (complete with cake board of the same size) on top of a smaller bowl or turntable.

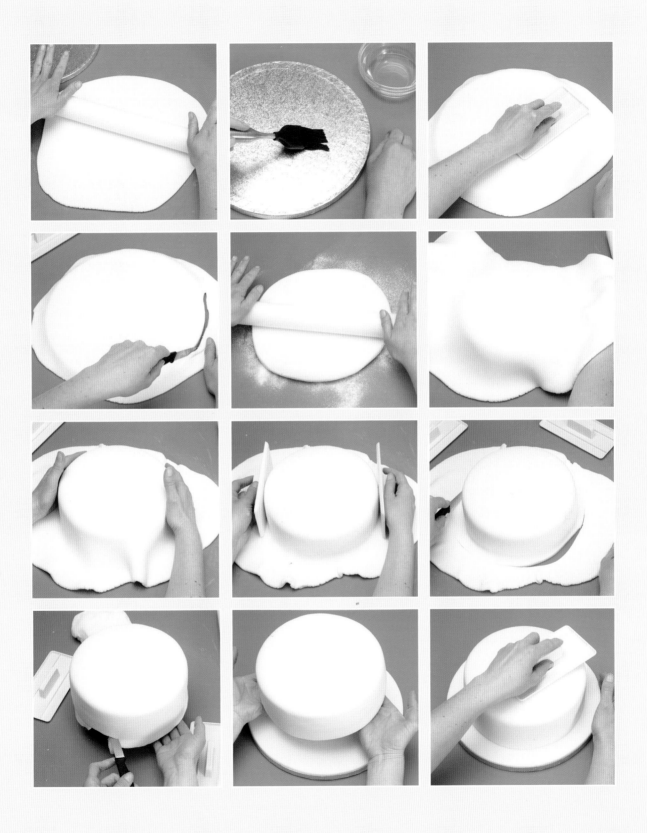

12 Run over the cake again with the cake smoother until the sugarpaste overhangs the cake board. Trim the icing flush with the bottom of the board. Smooth with your hand to leave a neat finish.

13 Place a little royal icing onto the covered cake drum/board and carefully place the cake on top. For vegan or egg-free cakes, put a small piece of sugarpaste in a dish with a drop of pre-boiled water. Warm in the microwave for a few seconds, stir and use this to stick the cake to the cake board.

14 Add any embossing or pattern while the icing is still soft. Leave to dry.

You can also use this method to cover a cake with chocolate paste.

Quantities to cover a cake and cake board with sugarpaste

	15cm (6")	20cm (8")	23cm (9")	25cm (10")	30cm (12")
ROUND	1kg (2lb 3oz)	1.5kg (3lb 5oz)	2kg (4lb 6oz)	2.5kg (5lb 8oz)	3kg (6lb 9oz)
SQUARE	1.25kg (2lb 12oz)	1.75kg (3lb 13oz)	2.25kg (4lb 15oz)	2.75kg (6lb 1oz)	3.25kg (7lb 2oz)

HOW TO MAKE A PAPER PIPING BAG

Small paper piping bags are used to pipe delicate or controlled patterns. They can be used with different shapes and sizes of nozzle to pipe icing, softened sugarpaste and buttercream or without a nozzle to pipe less delicate decoration such as chocolate.

You will need:

Greaseproof paper

Scissors

Piping nozzle

Royal icing

1 Cut a rectangle of greaseproof paper. The length should be three times the width.

2 Fold the paper from one corner to the opposite corner to make two long triangles. Cut along this line.

3 The point of the piping bag is along the long side of the triangle, opposite the point of the shortest side.

4 With the longest side furthest away from you, fold in the shortest side of the triangle to form a cone shape. Wrap around the rest of the triangle to form a cone.

5 Fold the two points inside the bag to secure the cone.

6 Snip off the tip of the bag and insert a piping nozzle.

7 After filling the piping bag with icing, fold over the top, then fold in the two sides and roll down the top of the piping bag.

DOWELLING GUIDE

Dowels are pushed into a cake at certain points to ensure stability if you are making a cake with two or more tiers. I recommend using wide, hollow American-style dowels to stack tiered cakes as special-diet cakes are softer than traditional versions and these dowels are more supportive than thinner ones.

You will need:

Cakes, covered/iced as required

Dowelling guide template (see page 163)

Modelling tool (any)

Hollow cake dowels

Pencil

Kitchen scissors or carving knife

1 Place the dowelling guide centrally onto the cake. Mark the position of each dowel using a modelling tool or the end of a paintbrush.

2 Remove the guide and push a dowel into the centre of the mark until it reaches the cake board. Mark on the dowel 1mm (under $^1/_8$") above where it meets the top of the cake, making sure the pencil does not come into contact with the cake covering. Repeat this at the other points.

3 Remove the dowels, find the mark furthest up the dowels and cut all five to the same length to ensure the tiers

are level. Use strong kitchen scissors or a carving knife to cut the dowels.

4 Insert the dowels back into the cake. Repeat with each cake, excluding the top tier.

5 For cakes containing egg, use a dab of royal icing between the dowels to stick the cake tiers together. To stick tiers of egg-free cakes together, put a small piece of sugarpaste in a dish with a drop of pre-boiled water. Warm in the microwave for a few seconds, stir and use straight away. After dowelling, pour onto the middle of the base tier and place the next cake tier on top. Repeat on any further tiers, excluding the top.

Projects

I have tried to show how different sugarcraft methods can be adapted to decorate cakes suitable for special diets. The instructions for each of these cakes are suitable for wheat-free, gluten-free, dairy-free, egg-free, vegan and nut-free cakes, except the croquembouche which contains egg.

For all projects, remember to check your ingredients are suitable for the diet you are catering for. Make sure the sugarpaste has not been used on other cakes; if you are not sure, use a fresh batch.

Animal Sugar Biscuits or Shortbread

I have piped around each of these biscuits with watered-down sugarpaste to give the finish of a royal iced run-out. This step can be omitted but gives a neat finish.

Edibles

Shortbread or sugar biscuit dough, see recipes on pages 62 and 64

Sugarpaste: black, brown, green, grey, red, white, yellow

Paste food colours: black, brown, dark green, red, yellow

Edible glue

Equipment

Basic equipment, see pages 26 to 27

Cookie cutters: elephant, giraffe, snake and crocodile (Wilton)

Piping nozzles: nos. 2 and 3

Stitching tool (PME)

Thick cocktail stick

Very small square and circle cutters

Use the animal-shaped cookie cutters to cut out the biscuits. Bake as per the recipe instructions and leave to cool.

Elephant

1 Roll out the grey sugarpaste to about 2mm (under ¼") thick.

2 Cut out elephants from the sugarpaste using the cookie cutter. Stick them to the biscuits with watered-down sugarpaste. Smooth over with your hand.

3 Mix ½tsp cooled, boiled water with 40g (1½oz) of the same grey sugarpaste or a contrasting colour. Paddle the sugarpaste on a plate with a small cranked palette knife to remove any lumps.

4 Fill a piping bag fitted with a no. 3 nozzle with the sugarpaste. Pipe around each elephant and leave to set. Pipe a tail with the same grey sugarpaste.

5 Mix ¼tsp cooled, boiled water with 20g (¾oz) white sugarpaste. Remove any lumps as before and use this to fill a piping bag fitted with a no. 2 nozzle.

6 Use the white sugarpaste to pipe the tusks, eyes and toes onto each elephant.

7 Roll out a small piece of grey sugarpaste and cut out the shape for the ear. Attach to each elephant using edible glue.

8 Mix ¼tsp cooled, boiled water with 20g (¾oz) black sugarpaste. Paddle the sugarpaste on a plate with a small cranked palette knife to remove any lumps. Use this to fill a piping bag fitted with a no. 2 nozzle.

9 Pipe black dots in the eyes.

Crocodile

1 Roll out the green sugarpaste to about 2mm (under ¼") thick.

2 Cut out several crocodiles from the sugarpaste using the cookie cutter. Stick them to the biscuits with watered-down sugarpaste. Smooth over with your hand.

3 Use the stitching tool to make the marks on the crocodiles' backs.

4 Use the cocktail stick to make the nostrils and lines on the feet.

5 Mix ½tsp cooled, boiled water with 40g (1½oz) of the same green sugarpaste. Pipe around each crocodile as for the elephants.

6 Pipe white dots for the eyes, then pipe black dots on the eyes and green for the eyelids.

Giraffe

1 Roll out the yellow sugarpaste to about 2mm (under ¼") thick.

2 Use the giraffe cookie cutter to cut out giraffes from the sugarpaste. Stick them onto the biscuits with watered-down sugarpaste. Smooth over with your hand.

3 Mix ½tsp cooled, boiled water with 40g (1½oz) of the same yellow sugarpaste. Pipe around the giraffes as before then pipe a tail and the ossicones (horns) on the giraffes' heads.

4 Roll out a small piece of brown sugarpaste thinly. Cut out lots of small squares and stick to the body of each giraffe.

5 Mix ¼tsp cooled, boiled water with 20g (¾oz) brown sugarpaste and use to pipe the top of the ossicones and the giraffes' manes.

6 Pipe white dots for the eyes, then pipe black dots on top.

Snake

1 Roll out the yellow sugarpaste to about 2mm (under ¼") thick.

2 Use the snake cutter to cut out snakes from the sugarpaste.

3 Stick to the cookies with watered-down sugarpaste. Smooth over with your hand.

4 Mix ½tsp cooled, boiled water with 40g (1½oz) of the same yellow sugarpaste and use to pipe around each snake.

5 Thinly roll out the red sugarpaste. Cut out small circles and stick to the snakes with edible glue. Cut a long, thin strip of red sugarpaste for the tongue and stick to the snakes with edible glue.

6 Pipe on eyes with watered-down white sugarpaste then dots of black sugarpaste.

Christmas Gingerbread

These biscuits can be stored in a cake tin or make lovely Christmas gifts when presented in small, cellophane bags tied with a ribbon. You could also decorate Christmas shortbread biscuits using the same method (see recipe on page 62).

Edibles

Gingerbread dough, see recipe on page 63

Sugarpaste: black, blue, green, red, white, yellow

Paste food colours: black, blue, dark green, orange, red

Fairy Sparkles Dust Food Colour: Ice White

Writing icing in different colours for decorating biscuits, or watered-down coloured sugarpaste in paper piping bags

Equipment

Basic equipment, see pages 26 to 27

Cutters: gingerbread man, Christmas tree, snowman, small triangle, small star

Piping nozzles: 3 x no. 3, no. 42 shell nozzle

Roll out the dough to 5mm (¼") thick. Cut out gingerbread men, Christmas trees and snowmen, bake as per the recipe and leave to cool.

Father Christmas

1 Roll out the red sugarpaste to 2mm (under ¼") thick.

2 Use the same cookie cutter as the dough to cut out gingerbread men from the red sugarpaste. Cut off the head and lower body so you are left with a jacket. Cut out triangles from the leftover paste for Santa's hat. Make the trousers in the same way from black sugarpaste. Stick them onto the gingerbread with watered-down sugarpaste. Smooth with your hand.

3 Mix 40g (1½oz) red sugarpaste with ½tsp of cooled, boiled water. Paddle the sugarpaste on a plate with a small cranked palette knife to remove any lumps. Fill a piping bag fitted with a no. 3 nozzle and pipe around the

TOP TIPS

If you want to hang the biscuits on the Christmas tree, pierce a hole at the top of each biscuit before baking. When decorated, thread a piece of ribbon through the hole and tie into a loop.

Do not store in a plastic container otherwise the icing will sweat.

jacket and hat. Do the same with black sugarpaste to outline the trousers. Leave to dry.

4 Mix 80g (2¾oz) white sugarpaste with 1tsp cooled, boiled water. Remove any lumps as before and fill a paper piping bag fitted with a no. 42 nozzle. Pipe a line down the centre of the jacket. Pipe shells around the top and bottom and on the cuffs of the jacket for fur.

5 Pipe a fur trim and bobble on the hat. Use the same piping bag to pipe the beard.

6 Pipe two black eyes with the writing icing. Leave the icing to set.

Christmas tree

1 Roll out the green sugarpaste to 2mm (under ¼") thick.

2 Use the same cookie cutter to cut out Christmas trees from the

green sugarpaste. Stick them onto the gingerbread with watered-down sugarpaste. Smooth with your hand.

3 Mix 40g (1½oz) green sugarpaste with ½tsp cooled, boiled water and pipe around the Christmas trees. Leave to dry.

4 When dry, brush with Ice White Fairy Sparkles dust using a dry, flat paintbrush.

5 Cut out small stars from the yellow sugarpaste and stick to the top of the trees with a little cooled, boiled water.

6 Decorate the biscuits with watered-down coloured sugarpaste in paper piping bags or the tubes of writing icing.

Snowman

1 Roll out the white sugarpaste to 2mm (under ¼") thick.

2 Use the same cookie cutter to cut out snowmen from the white sugarpaste. Stick them onto the gingerbread with watered-down sugarpaste. Smooth with your hand. Mark dots for the mouth with a cocktail stick.

3 Brush with Ice White Fairy Sparkles dust using a dry, flat paintbrush.

4 Mix 40g (1½oz) white sugarpaste with ½tsp cooled, boiled water and pipe around the snowmen. Leave to dry.

5 Roll a tiny orange sugarpaste carrot shape for the nose.

6 Pipe eyes and buttons with black writing icing or watered-down black sugarpaste.

7 Cut out the shape for the hat and scarf from blue sugarpaste and stick these to the snowmen with cooled, boiled water using a small paintbrush. Leave to dry.

Butterfly Cakes

There are plenty of recipe books featuring cupcakes but I've chosen to champion the humble butterfly cake. When I made these for a vegan and gluten-free stall at a food festival, they were a huge hit – many people with special diets told me they hadn't been able to eat one since their childhood. Finish the cakes as close to serving as possible to prevent the 'wings' from drying out.

Edibles

One quantity gluten-free or vegan vanilla sponge, see recipes on pages 44 and 69

Buttercream or dairy-free buttercream, see recipes on pages 87 and 88

Paste food colour: pink

Crystallised violets

Crystallised rose fragments

Icing sugar in a shaker

Equipment

Basic equipment, see pages 26 to 27

Dotty cupcake cases and mini cupcake cases: blue, pink (SK)

Large nylon piping bag fitted with a large star-shaped nozzle

If using the gluten-free vanilla sponge, this recipe should make 18 cupcakes or about 80 mini cupcakes. Make sure to fill the cupcake cases only ¾ full.

If using the vegan vanilla sponge, this recipe makes 27 cupcakes and about 100 mini cupcakes.

1 Bake the cupcakes in the pink and blue dotty cases. When baked, cut the top off each cupcake and cut each top in half.

2 Colour half of the buttercream pink.

3 Using the nylon piping bag fitted with a star-shaped nozzle, pipe a swirl of buttercream on top of each cupcake. Use pink buttercream for the cupcakes in blue cases and cream for the cupcakes in pink cases. Stick the rounded side of two 'wings' into the buttercream on each cupcake.

4 Pipe a small swirl of buttercream in the centre of each pair of wings. Dust with icing sugar.

5 Place a crystallised violet on top of the pink swirl of buttercream and crystallised rose fragments on top of the plain-coloured buttercream. Alternatively, you can crystallise your own edible flowers (see page 118).

Egg-free Crystallised Edible Flowers

If you are making your own crystallised flowers, make these in advance and allow to dry before use.

You will need

Edible flowers, such as borage, pansies, violets, rose petals, primrose, sweet peas

10g (¼oz) gum arabic

2tsp rose water

Caster sugar

Tray lined with greaseproof paper

1 Dissolve the gum arabic in the rose water and leave to stand for a few hours before use.

2 Use a small brush to paint the flowers one at a time with gum arabic.

3 Hold the flower over a bowl of sugar and sprinkle the sugar over the flower until it is evenly covered.

4 Leave to dry overnight on greaseproof paper.

Winter Wedding Cake

A range of allergen-free decoration has been used on this cake where traditionally egg- and gelatine-based decoration would be used. Make the wired poinsettias in advance so that you can simply place them on the cake when needed.

Edibles

15cm, 23cm and 30cm (6", 9" and 12") round cakes, prepared and filled on cake boards of the same size, covered with white sugarpaste

Flower paste: white

Sugarpaste: white

Modelling paste (half flower paste and half sugarpaste): white

Paste food colours: Daffodil (yellow), Holly/Ivy (dark green), Poinsettia (Christmas red)

Fairy Sparkles Dust Food Colour: Ice White

Dust food colours: Holly/Ivy (dark green), Poinsettia (Christmas red)

Edible glue

Rose water

Equipment

Basic equipment, see pages 26 to 27

38cm (15") round cake drum/board

28-gauge floral wires: white

Floral tape: moss green

Poinsettia cutters (FMM)

Large Poinsettia veiner (SK-GI)

Three sizes of calyx cutter

Multi ribbon cutter (FMM)

Piping nozzles: 2 x no. 1

Posy pick

15mm (⁵/₈") width ribbon: red

1 Cut seven 28-gauge wires into four equal lengths each.

2 Make a tiny hook at one end of five of the wires.

3 Roll a tiny ball of Holly/Ivy-coloured flower paste onto each hook. Shape into an oval. Snip the end of each oval with a pair of small pointed scissors.

4 Wrap the wires together with green floral tape starting at the bottom of the buds. Dust the tip of each bud with Poinsettia dust colour.

5 Roll a small ball of flower paste coloured with Poinsettia paste colour onto a wire. Roll into a sausage shape thin enough to just coat the wire the same length as the bract. Place

119

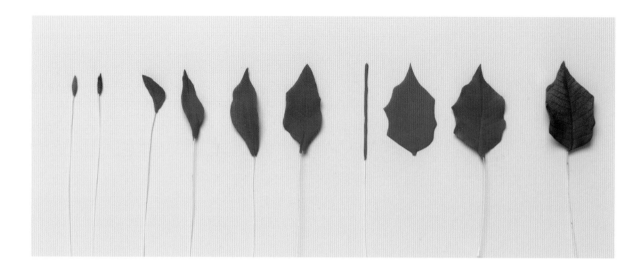

under a Flexi-Mat to prevent drying out. Do the same with the rest of the wires.

6 Roll out the Poinsettia-coloured flower paste thinly.

7 Cut out the bracts with the poinsettia cutters. You will need three of the smallest size, five of the next size up, five of the middle size, three of the second largest size and five of the largest size. Place under the Flexi-Mat.

8 Starting with the smallest, place a bract on the top-facing side of the Great Impressions Poinsettia veiner and place a coated wire centrally on top. Press with the other side of the veiner. The wire should stick to the bract. Soften the edges with a ball tool on top of a foam pad. Bend into shape.

9 Continue with the other bracts. Dust with Poinsettia dust colour and tape together while the paste is still soft so the bracts can be shaped.

10 Starting with the smallest bract, tape this at the bottom of the bud with green floral tape. Tape another bract the same size next to this. Continue this with all the bracts, going up in size.

11 Bend the bracts into shape. Pass through the steam of a kettle to set the colour.

12 For the green bracts, cut two 28-gauge wires into three pieces. Roll a ball of Holly/Ivy-coloured flower paste onto the wires and roll into a sausage shape thin enough to just coat the wire the same length as the bract. Place under the Flexi-Mat.

13 Roll out the Holly/Ivy coloured flower paste thinly. Cut out six bracts using the largest cutter.

14 Place a bract onto the top-facing side of the Great Impressions Poinsettia veiner, then place a coated wire centrally on top. Press with the other

side of the veiner. The wire should stick to the bract. Soften the edges with a ball tool on top of a foam pad. Bend into shape.

15 Dust with Holly/Ivy dust colour.

16 Tape the green bracts underneath the red bracts while still soft. Bend into shape. Pass through the steam of a kettle to set the colour and leave to dry.

17 Make two more poinsettias and leave to dry.

18 Cover the cake drum with white sugarpaste and stick centrally on top of the 30cm (12") cake.

19 Using the dowelling guide, insert dowels into the 30cm and 23cm (12" and 9") cakes.

20 Stack the cakes, sticking them together with the melted sugarpaste.

21 To make the mini poinsettias, roll out the Poinsettia-coloured flower paste as thin as possible. Cut out several calyces in all three sizes. Roll gently over the paste from side to side with a cocktail stick pointed to the centre to widen it slightly.

22 Stick two large calyces together with edible glue, placing the points of the top calyx between the points of the bottom calyx. Do the same with all the calyces.

23 Place each flower on a foam pad and push into the centre with a ball tool. Leave to dry on a piece of foam.

24 For the ribbon, roll the red modelling paste into a long sausage. Roll flat with a rolling pin.

25 Using the multi ribbon cutter set at a 1.5cm (about ½") width, cut out a strip long enough to wrap around the 30cm (12") cake. Stick around the base of the cake with rose water. Repeat for the other two cakes.

26 Cut a strip of modelling paste 23cm (9") long to make a bow loop. Fold the two ends into the centre and stick with rose water. Hold the shape with pieces of cotton wool. Make two more bows with a strip 20cm (8") long and 18cm (7") long. Leave to dry slightly until it holds its shape.

27 To let down the sugarpaste for piping, mix 20g (¾oz) white sugarpaste with ¼tsp cooled, boiled water. Paddle with a small palette knife on a plate and use to fill a piping bag fitted with a no. 1 nozzle.

28 Use the let-down sugarpaste to stick the bows onto each ribbon with the smallest bow on the top tier and the longest on the bottom tier. Stick a small strip of modelling paste over the join for the bow centre.

29 Attach the three sizes of mini poinsettias to the sides of the cakes with the let-down sugarpaste.

30 Pipe snowflakes and small dots around the mini poinsettias using the let-down white sugarpaste. Dab on the Fairy Sparkles dust with a paintbrush while the icing is still wet.

31 Mix 20g (¾oz) yellow sugarpaste with ¼tsp cooled, boiled water. Paddle on a plate and fill a piping bag fitted with a no. 1 nozzle.

32 Pipe five yellow dots in the centre of each flower.

33 Tape the three poinsettias together. Place a posy pick into the centre of the top cake and place the stems into this.

34 Attach a red ribbon around the sides of the cake board.

Individual Christmas Puddings

Gone are the days when you couldn't have a Christmas cake when on a special diet.
Making individual cakes also means you don't have to share!

Edibles

One quantity of fruit cake suitable for the special diet you are following, see recipes on pages 40, 52 and 74

Brandy

1.2kg (2lb 10oz) marzipan or nut-free 'marzipan' (see recipe on page 93)

Sugarpaste: 200g (7oz) white, 1.5kg (3lb 4oz) coloured with brown paste colour

A small amount of vegan and gluten-free flower paste

Paste food colours: black, brown, dark green, red, yellow

Equipment

Basic equipment, see pages 26 to 27

Half-sphere silicone mould

7.5cm (3") round cake cards

Circle cutters: 5cm (2"), plus 2 very small sizes

Small holly leaf cutter

Rose leaf veiner (SK-GI)

Makes 15 individual puddings

1 Make the fruit cake mix as per your chosen recipe. Pour into the half-sphere silicone moulds. Bake for 1 hour at 150°C/300°F/gas mark 2 or until a knife inserted comes out clean.

2 When cold, you can decorate the cakes. Loosen the fruit cake halves from the mould then put them back in the mould and trim the top off each cake. Use the top of the cake mould as a guide.

3 Brush the tops of the cakes with brandy. Take the cakes out of the mould.

4 Roll out ¼ the marzipan 5mm (¼") thick. Using the 5cm (2") round cutter, cut out 15 circles. Place the circles on half of the cakes. Smooth over and place another cake half on top. Smooth the join.

5 Brush the cakes with brandy.

6 Roll out the remaining marzipan to 5mm (¼") thick and cut out circles about 10cm (4") in diameter. Lift over each cake then smooth the marzipan onto the top and sides of the cake. If the marzipan creases, pull it away from the cake and push back on so that it is smooth.

7 Use the cake smoother to smooth the marzipan on the cake. Trim the marzipan from the bottom of the cakes with a sharp knife. Leave to dry for five days unless using vegan fruit cakes: these can be iced straight away as they will only keep for a week.

8 Brush the marzipanned fruit cakes with brandy.

9 Knead the brown sugarpaste until smooth. Dust the worktop with icing sugar and roll out the sugarpaste to 5mm (¼") thick.

10 Cut out circles that are 10cm (4") in diameter. Lift the icing over each cake then smooth onto the top and around the sides of the cake. If the icing forms

a crease, pull this away from the cake, straighten it out and push back onto the cake. Cut away the excess sugarpaste around the bottom of the cake and smooth with a cake smoother.

11 Measure how big the 'poured brandy sauce' will be on top of each cake. Roll out the white sugarpaste and cut out circles this size. Cut the shape of the poured sauce from this. Brush the top of the cake with a little cooled, boiled water and stick white icing to the top of the cake. Smooth over the icing with a cake smoother.

12 Roll out the red-coloured sugarpaste thinly. Cut out shapes with the larger of the small circle

cutters and stick randomly to the brown sugarpaste with edible glue.

13 Roll out the yellow-coloured sugarpaste thinly. Cut out shapes with the smaller of the small circle cutters and stick randomly to the brown sugarpaste with edible glue. Repeat with the black-coloured sugarpaste.

14 Roll out the green flower paste and cut out three holly leaves. Mark the veins with the rose leaf veiner, bend into shape and leave to dry. When dry, stick to the top of the cake with edible glue. For the holly berries, roll three tiny balls of red sugarpaste and stick them where the leaves meet in the centre.

Dairy-free or Vegan Chocolate Gerbera Wedding Cake

If you are following a dairy-free or vegan diet you can still have an elegant chocolate wedding cake. The dairy-free ganache can also be used for piping using large Savoy piping nozzles in the same way as if it were chocolate ganache containing dairy. Leave the ganache overnight at room temperature to set before using for piping.

Edibles

One quantity of dairy-free or nut-free chocolate ganache (also suitable for vegans), see recipes on page 36

4kg (8lb 13oz) plain chocolate paste (to cover the cakes and board), plus a little extra for decorations, see recipe on page 95

15cm, 23cm and 30cm (6", 9" and 12") round cakes, covered with plain chocolate modelling paste

500g (1lb 1oz) white chocolate modelling paste coloured with a mixture of Marigold (tangerine) paste colour and orange dust colour*

Small amount white chocolate modelling paste coloured with yellow paste colour

Edible glue

*It is important to use a mixture of paste and dust colours because paste colour alone will make the chocolate paste too wet.

Equipment

Basic equipment, see pages 26 to 27

38cm (15") round cake drum/board covered with plain chocolate paste

Decorative yellow ribbon

Multi petal cutters: 70mm and 105mm (2¾ and 4") (Orchard Products)

Large carnation cutter (Orchard Products)

1 Place the prepared stacked cake and covered base board on a cooling rack over a sheet of baking parchment large enough to catch any overflowing ganache.

2 Prepare the dairy-free ganache following the recipe on page 36. Leave to cool to 32°C, stirring occasionally.

3 Pour the ganache over the cake from the top and keep pouring until it completely covers the sides of all of the cakes and the cake board.

4 Pop any air bubbles with a thin cocktail stick. Leave the cake on the cooling rack for a day to allow the ganache to set. Do not move the cake until the ganache has set.

5 When the ganache has set, clean the edge of the cake drum.

6 Attach a length of ribbon around the base of each cake and the cake drum.

The ganache will dry matt: I have tried adding glucose syrup or vegetable fat to give the ganache a shine but this doesn't make any difference. The finished effect looks similar to the chocolate paste covering so you can omit the ganache if you need to save time.

7 Roll out the orange-coloured chocolate paste and cut out 12 large gerberas. Use a fine paintbrush to push the petals out of the cutter.

8 Make two long indents in each petal with a thick cocktail stick or the end of a thin paintbrush.

9 Stick two sets of petals together with edible glue. The top row of petals should sit in between the bottom petals.

10 Roll out more orange-coloured paste and cut out six smaller gerberas. Indent the petals as before and stick one centrally on top of each large gerbera.

11 Make balls of yellow-coloured chocolate paste for the flower centre. Squash the balls to flatten them and snip all over the top with pointed scissors.

12 Roll out more orange-coloured chocolate paste and cut out 12 carnations. Frill the edges with a cocktail stick.

13 Brush half the carnations with edible glue, sit a yellow flower centre on top and bring up the orange paste around the sides. Sit this on top of another frilled, glued carnation and bring up the paste around the sides.

14 Stick a centre onto each flower with edible glue.

15 Make a small pyramid shape of plain chocolate paste. Stick this centrally on top of the cake. Stick three gerberas to this and arrange to hide the pyramid.

16 Arrange the remaining three gerberas on the cake and stick in place with melted chocolate.

Dairy-free White Chocolate Rose Cake

When I first made this cake, many people didn't realise you could buy dairy-free white chocolate. This became a popular wedding cake, especially with vegans.

Edibles

15cm and 23cm (6" and 9") round cakes on cake boards the same size

30cm (12") round cake on a 30cm (12") cake drum/board

Dairy-free white chocolate paste: 4.8kg (8lb 13oz) for the roses, 3.2kg (6lb 9oz) to cover all three cakes and the cake drum/board (see page 95)

800g (1lb 12oz) dairy-free white chocolate for the frill and to secure the roses

Edible glue

When preparing the cakes, remember to use nut-free recipes and fillings if the cake is to be suitable for a nut-free diet.

Equipment

Basic equipment, see pages 26 to 27

38cm (15") round cake drum/board

25cm (10") round x 5cm (2") deep polystyrene cake dummy

50mm (2") rose petal cutter (Tinkertech Two) or circle cutter

8.5cm (3½") round cutter for the three large roses

Large rose leaf cutter (Orchard Products)

Rose leaf veiner (SK-GI)

Marble chopping board that will fit in the freezer

Baking tray lined with baking parchment

Pair of cotton or vinyl gloves (I try not to use latex gloves as many people are allergic to latex)

Chocolate roses

1 Roll out the paste and cut out 11 petals for each rose. Use a small paintbrush to push the petal out of the cutter. Pull up the trimmings, roll them into a ball and keep covered to use again.

2 Lightly knead a hand-sized ball of white chocolate paste and mould part of this into a cone shape ²/₃ the length of the petal cutter, keeping this attached to the ball of paste.

3 Brush the base of each petal with edible glue. Wrap one petal around the top of the cone, completely covering the tip. Half-wrap a petal around the cone at the same height as the first petal, then wrap another petal opposite and link them together to form a bud.

4 Wrap a layer of three petals around the cone and pull out the very top of each petal. Add another layer of five petals. Pull out and shape the petals. Use your fingers to shape the

TOP TIP

Make the roses the day before, attaching them to the cake when they have hardened a little but will still move so the petals can be adjusted on the cake. About 120 should cover all three cakes, depending on size. The chocolate paste doesn't dry out very quickly so you can roll out as much as you can manage at one time.

bottom of the rose and cut off the base with scissors. Leave to dry.

5 Make three large roses the same way using the large circle cutter. If they don't hold their shape, place them in bowls until set. Cut out a calyx for each of the three large roses.

Cakes

6 Cover the cake board and the prepared cakes with dairy-free white chocolate paste 5mm (¼") thick.

7 Water down a little chocolate paste to a spreading consistency with cooled, boiled water. Spread this over the sides of the cake dummy but not the top.

8 Knead and roll out 500g (1lb 1oz) chocolate paste and cover the cake dummy. Smooth over the sides. Carve

the chocolate paste off the top, flush with the top of the cake dummy. Mix a small ball of chocolate paste with a drop of pre-boiled water and melt in the microwave for a few seconds. Use this to stick the cake dummy centrally to the 38cm (15") cake board.

9 Dowel the 30cm and 23cm (12" and 9") cakes using the guide on page 163.

Chocolate frills

10 Temper half the white chocolate in a microwave. Break up the chocolate into a large glass bowl, place in the microwave on a low setting and stir every 30 seconds until the chocolate has just melted. If there are a few bits of chocolate that have not melted, do not heat any more but leave to melt, stirring occasionally.

11 Wearing cotton or vinyl gloves,

take the marble chopping board from the freezer.

12 Working quickly, spread a line of chocolate with a palette knife over the top of the chopping board.

13 Trim one long edge with a sharp knife so the strip is about 3.5cm (1½") wide.

14 Run a clean palette knife under the chocolate, pick it up and quickly mould it into a frill shape. Place on a baking tray lined with baking parchment.

15 Spread another line of chocolate under the first and repeat this step. Work down the chopping board until the board gets too warm to work with. Leave the chocolate frills to set.

16 Place the chopping board back

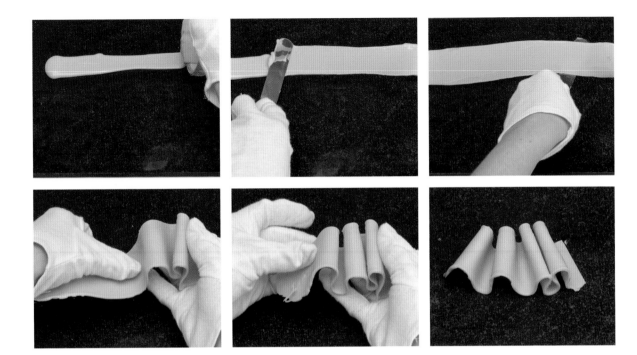

into the freezer again. If you have another marble tile or chopping board, keep one in the freezer at all times so you can continue making frills.

17 When you have enough frills, fill a paper piping bag with melted dairy-free white chocolate. Stick a layer of frills onto the cake board around the dummy using the melted chocolate. Use a dry paintbrush to remove any drips of chocolate. Add another layer, ensuring it lies a little lower than the top of the cake dummy.

18 Mix a ball of chocolate paste with a drop of pre-boiled water and melt in the microwave for a few seconds.

Assembly

19 When the frill has set, secure the 30cm (12") cake on top of the cake dummy with a little of the melted chocolate paste.

20 Stick the 23cm (9") cake on top of this then secure the 15cm (6") cake on the top using melted chocolate paste.

21 Leave the cakes overnight to set.

22 Melt 50g (2oz) dairy-free white chocolate in the microwave and use this to fill a paper piping bag. Starting with the bottom row, stick two rows of roses to the 30cm (12") cake with the melted chocolate.

23 Roll out some white chocolate paste and cut out lots of rose leaves, then push the chocolate paste out of the cutter using a small paintbrush. Mark each leaf with the rose leaf veiner.

24 Stick a row of leaves over the edge of the 30cm (12") cake, half-covering the edge of the cake and the

rest covering the side of the top row of roses. Overlap the leaves slightly.

25 Add another row of leaves starting from the bottom edge of the next cake so they slightly overlap the first layer, completely covering the top edge of the 30cm (12") cake.

26 Stick two rows of roses to the side of the 23cm (9") cake. Cover the top of this cake with two more rows of rose leaves.

27 Secure another two rows of roses to the side of the 15cm (6") cake then completely cover the top of the cake with chocolate rose leaves, starting with a row around the outside edge and continuing towards the centre.

28 Place the three large roses on the top of the cake. Secure with melted chocolate.

Wheat-, Gluten- and Dairy-free Croquembouche

This is one type of dessert which many people on a special diet never dreamt they could eat. A smaller version can be made as a dinner party dessert.

Edibles

48 profiteroles, see pages 60 to 61

3 quantities dairy- and gluten-free pastry cream, see page 90, or dairy-free whipping cream

500g (1lb 1oz) caster or granulated white sugar

Equipment

Basic equipment, see pages 26 to 27

A croquembouche mould or an A1 sheet of thick card rolled into a cone

Baking parchment

Serves 16

1 Fit a nylon piping bag with a small round nozzle and fill with the cold pastry cream or whipped dairy-free cream. You could also use a mixture of both.

2 Pipe the pastry cream or cream into each profiterole and store in the fridge until required.

3 If using card as a mould, roll it into a cone and stick together with tape. Line the outside of the cone with baking parchment to prevent the card from sticking to the profiteroles.

4 When you are ready to assemble the croquembouche, make the caramel. Pour 500g (1lb 1oz) white sugar into a heavy-based saucepan. Add enough water to moisten the sugar.

5 Place on the heat and stir to dissolve the sugar. Once the syrup is boiling do not stir as it will cause the syrup to crystallise.

6 Dip a clean pastry brush into a cup of water and brush down the inside of the saucepan to wash any sugar crystals into the syrup.

7 Fill a sink with cold water.

8 Boil the syrup until it turns a golden caramel colour. If one part colours before the rest, lightly swirl the saucepan to mix; don't stir it. Quickly dip the base of the saucepan into the cold water to stop the caramel cooking.

9 Briefly dip the top of the first profiterole into the caramel and place at the bottom of the cone. Continue dipping the profiteroles into the caramel and stack around the outside of the cone with the top of the profiterole facing outwards until the cone is completely covered. If the caramel becomes hard, melt it over a low

TOP TIP

The profiteroles can be made in advance and frozen unfilled until needed. Fill the profiteroles as close to serving as possible (they will go soggy if filled too early). For food safety reasons, the Croquembouche should be constructed within four hours of serving because it cannot be stored in the fridge due to the moisture, which would melt the caramel.

heat, swirl the pan gently; don't stir or the caramel can crystallise. Leave the croquembouche to set for a few minutes before teasing out the cone. Place the croquembouche onto a serving plate.

10 To decorate with spun sugar, just before serving have a rolling pin and large spoon or whisk to hand.

11 Pour 200g (7oz) white sugar into a heavy-based saucepan and make caramel as above.

12 While the caramel is quite fluid, dip the spoon or whisk in and flick the caramel backwards and forwards over the rolling pin to produce long strands of caramel. (This can be quite messy so protect your kitchen floor and surfaces with paper.) Wrap these around the croquembouche whilst they are still warm and flexible. Repeat until it is completely covered. If the caramel becomes hard, melt it over a low heat and swirl the pan gently.

TOP TIP

This dessert is also a good option for diabetics. Fill the profiteroles with unsweetened whipped cream and dip them in plain chocolate instead of caramel.

Individual Cakes with Personalised Rings

This design shows how versatile piping with let-down sugarpaste can be. For piping long lines down the side of a cake, I would use American frosting instead as it has more stretch than sugarpaste.

Edibles

15cm (6") round cake covered with white sugarpaste, on a cake board the same size

25 x 5cm (2") round cakes covered with white sugarpaste

Vegan and gluten-free flower paste: white

Sugarpaste: white

Paste food colours: blue, Holly/Ivy (dark green)

Metallic lustre dust food colour: silver

Edible glue

Vegan vodka or rose water (if you keep a bottle and brush with this, ensure it has not been used on pastes containing egg or dairy)

Makes 15 individual cakes and a 15cm (6") cake

Equipment

Basic equipment, see pages 26 to 27

Multi-ribbon cutter (FMM)

Piping nozzle: no. 2 (PME)

Biscuit letter embosser

2 wide dowels

Blossom cutters: 6mm plunger cutter (PME) and 15mm metal cutter (Tinkertech Two)

Rose petal cutters: 45mm and 50mm (Tinkertech Two)

20-gauge floral wire

Floral tape: dark green

15mm (5/8") width ribbon: blue

Tealight

Posy pick

Rings

1 For the rings, slide the letters for one name into the embosser. Rub a thin layer of white vegetable fat over the outside of an American-style wide cake dowel to mould the rings around.

2 Roll out the flower paste wide enough to wrap around a dowel and long enough to cut 25 strips from.

3 Emboss the name at the top of the flower paste, leave a space then emboss the name again underneath. Continue as many times as will fit.

4 Set the multi-ribbon cutter to the widest setting without using any spacers, around 1cm (3/8") wide.

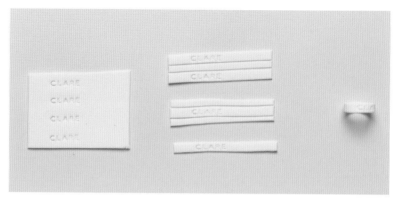

5 Cut a strip of the paste using the multi ribbon cutter keeping the name in the centre. Measure around the dowel and cut the strips of flower paste to this length. Wrap around the dowel, sealing the join with your fingers, and neaten before leaving to dry.

6 Follow these steps with the other name. Leave to dry.

7 Slide off the dowel and leave to dry thoroughly.

8 Once dry, paint with silver lustre dust mixed with a drop of vodka or rose water. I find it best to apply two or three thin coats of silver to the rings, leaving to dry between coats.

Roses

9 Cut five 20-gauge wires into three equal lengths. Make a small hook at one end of each wire using a pair of long-nosed pliers kept just for sugarcraft.

10 Roll 11 equal-sized cones of flower paste about 5g (just under ¼oz) each. They need to be ¾ the length of the petal cutter you are using.

11 Light a tealight. Hold the hook of a wire over the tealight until hot then stick into the bottom of a cone of flower paste straight away so that the sugar bonds onto the hot wire. Do this with the other wires. Leave to dry.

12 Roll out the white flower paste as thinly as possible.

13 Cut out 11 smaller rose petals and five larger rose petals for each full flower. Cover with a Flexi-Mat to prevent them from drying.

14 Soften the edge of the smaller petals on a foam pad using a ball tool.

15 Brush two petals with edible glue and wrap these tightly around the bud, interlinking them with the tip of the petals raised 2mm (under ¼") higher than the tip of the cone and completely covering the cone.

16 Turn the remaining nine petals over. Brush along the base of each petal with edible glue.

17 Wrap three more petals around the cone quite tightly, interlinking the petals.

18 Add two more layers of three petals around the cone, wrapping each layer a little looser. Shape the tips of the petals with your fingers.

19 Soften the edge of the larger petals on a foam pad using a ball tool.

20 Turn the petals over and brush the base with edible glue. Wrap all five petals in one layer around the rose. Shape the tip of the petals with your fingers. Leave to dry.

21 Make nine roses in this way.

Rose buds

22 To make the rose buds, roll out the flower paste as thin as possible and cut out eight 45mm (1¾") petals for each bud. Cover with a Flexi-Mat to prevent drying.

23 Soften the edge of the petals on a foam pad using a ball tool.

24 Brush two petals with edible glue and wrap these tightly around the bud, interlinking them with the tip of the petals raised 2mm (under ¼") higher

than the tip of the cone and completely covering the cone.

25 Turn the remaining six petals over. Brush along the edge of each petal with edible glue.

26 Wrap three more petals around the cone quite tightly, interlinking the petals.

27 Add the last layer of three petals around the cone, wrapping each layer a little looser. Shape the tips of the petals with your fingers.

28 Roll out a small ball of flower paste coloured with Holly/Ivy paste colour as thin as you can. Cut out 11 calyces.

29 Soften the edges and make cuts into the sides to resemble a real rose calyx. Turn upside down and brush with edible glue.

30 Push the rose wire through the centre of the calyx and stick to the bottom of the rose. Roll a tiny ball of green flower paste and stick this underneath the calyx.

31 Wrap the rose wires with dark green floral tape to completely cover them.

Cakes

32 For the cakes, colour 40g (1½oz) sugarpaste with blue paste colour. Mix with ½tsp cooled, boiled water. Use a small cranked palette knife to paddle the sugarpaste on a plate to get rid of any lumps. Use this to fill a paper piping bag fitted with a no. 2 nozzle.

33 Attach a length of 15mm (⁵/₈") width blue ribbon around the base of each small cake. Secure with a dot of let-down sugarpaste at the join.

34 For half the cakes, pipe a 2cm (¾") long line vertically down the side of the cake to the ribbon. Pipe another line the same length about 1.5cm (½") away. Pipe two shorter lines in between at equal distances. Continue this pattern around the cake.

35 Finely roll out the blue flower paste. Cut out lots of tiny blossoms and 12 larger blossoms. Place on a foam pad and soften the petals of the larger blossom with a ball tool. Push into the centre with the ball tool of all the blossoms.

36 Roll out some white flower paste thinly. Cut out tiny blossoms. Place onto a foam pad and push a ball tool into the centre.

37 Stick tiny blue blossoms above the shorter lines with edible glue.

38 Fill a small piping bag with 20g (¾oz) white sugarpaste let down with ¼tsp cooled, boiled water. Snip the tip off the bag. Pipe a centre in each blossom.

39 Stick white and blue tiny blossoms randomly around the rest of the individual cakes. Pipe a white centre in the blue blossoms and a blue centre in the white blossoms.

40 Place the two rings on top of each cake, with one on top of the other. Stick with let-down white sugarpaste.

41 Copy this pattern on the sides of the 15cm (6") cake with wider spaces between the lines. It may be easier to place the cake on a tilted turntable to pipe the lines.

42 Stick the large blue blossoms above the shorter piped lines.

43 Place a posy pick into the centre of the top of the cake. Arrange the roses on top of the cake, setting the wires into the posy pick.

Important note: Remember to remove the wired flowers before the cake is served.

Traditional Bakery-style Cake

The pattern on this cake is piped with American frosting. This can be used to create many decorations which would normally be achieved with royal icing.

Edibles

20cm (8") square cake covered with white sugarpaste, sitting on a 28cm (11") square cake drum/board also covered with sugarpaste

½ quantity of American frosting, see recipe on page 89

Paste food colour: violet

Equipment

Basic equipment, see pages 26 to 27

Baking parchment cut into 2.5cm (1") squares

Flower nail

Piping nozzles: no. 1, no. 6 star, no. 58 petal (left- or right-handed)

4cm (1½") width ribbon: lilac

15mm (⅝") width ribbon: lilac

Piped flowers

1 Colour the American frosting with violet paste colour. Fit a piping bag with a petal nozzle and fill with the frosting.

2 Stick a small square of baking parchment to the flower nail with a dot of frosting.

3 Pipe five petals, one at a time, twisting the flower nail around as you pipe each petal.

4 Finish by piping three dots into the centre of the flower with a contrasting colour. Take the square of greaseproof paper off the nail and leave the flower to set before removing from the greaseproof paper, ready for use. Repeat to make approximately 12 flowers.

Cake

5 Make a small mark at the four corners of the cake using a scriber or modelling tool. Measure the length between the marks along the sides of the cake and mark the centre.

6 Score a 10cm (4") square centrally on the cake then another square 13cm (5") wide. Place the cake onto a turntable.

7 Fill a piping bag fitted with a no. 1 nozzle with white frosting. Pipe tiny scrolls along the 10cm (4") square line.

8 Fill a piping bag fitted with a no. 1 nozzle with lilac-coloured frosting. Use this to pipe tiny scrolls along the 13cm (5") square.

9 Pipe your chosen message in the centre of the cake with the coloured frosting.

10 Fit a piping bag with a no. 6 star-shaped nozzle and fill with white frosting.

11 Pipe shells around the bottom edge of the cake then pipe scrolls around the top edge of the cake. Stick the piped flowers to the cake.

12 Wrap the wide ribbon around the cake and tie into a bow at the front. Stick a length of 15mm (¾") ribbon around the sides of the cake drum to finish.

Daisy Chain Christening Cake

This popular christening cake uses simple drop piping with sugarpaste to great effect.
Make the daisies in advance so they have time to dry.

Edibles

20cm (8") round cake covered with white sugarpaste on a 28cm (11") cake drum/board covered with white sugarpaste

Vegan and gluten-free flower paste, see recipe on page 93

¼ quantity of vegan and wheat-free pastillage, see page 94

Paste food colours: green, yellow

Sugarpaste: 20g (1½oz) green, 40g (1½oz) white, 10g (¼oz) yellow

Icing sugar in a shaker

Equipment

Basic equipment, see pages 26 to 27

Daisy cutters: large and small (FMM)

Piping nozzles: no. 1, 3, 6 star-shaped

Decorative plaque cutter (Orchard Products Plaque 1)

1.5cm (½") heart cutter (PME)

15mm (⁵/₈") width ribbon: yellow

1 Dust the worktop with icing sugar and roll out the flower paste finely.

2 Cut out 17 large daisies and six small daisies for the card. Push the flower paste out of the cutter using a small paintbrush. Place on a foam pad and run the ball tool from the end of each petal towards the centre. Leave to dry on a dimpled piece of foam if you have one.

3 Once dry, mix 20g (¾oz) yellow-coloured sugarpaste with ¼tsp cooled, boiled water. Paddle the sugarpaste on a plate with a small cranked palette knife to remove any lumps. Use to fill a paper piping bag, snip off the tip of the bag and pipe the centres of the daisies.

4 To make the pastillage plaque, roll out the pastillage and cut out two card shapes. Cut out two small hearts at the top of each plaque for the ribbon to be threaded through.

5 When the pastillage is dry, pipe on the baby's name with the coloured, watered-down sugarpaste. Stick the daisies around two corners of the plaque. Thread a piece of thin ribbon through the hearts to join the pieces together.

TOP TIP Allow the pastillage plaque to dry for three or four days on a wooden chopping board or a piece of cardboard until fully dry.

6 Cut a piece of greaseproof paper the same height as the cake and long enough to wrap around the outside.

7 Draw a line on the paper 3.5cm (1½") down from the top.

8 Place a 7cm (2¾") wide cookie cutter on the line and draw around it to make a semicircle. Move the cutter along so it is touching the last semicircle and continue along the line. You should end up with 10 semicircles along the strip. Cut these out of the paper.

9 Wrap the strip around the cake with the semicircles at the top. Scribe the cake along each cut out semicircle.

10 Mix 20g (¾oz) green sugarpaste with ¼tsp cooled, boiled water. Paddle the sugarpaste on a plate with a small cranked palette knife to remove any lumps. Use this to fill a piping bag fitted with a no. 3 nozzle.

11 Put the cake on a tilted turntable or prop up one side of the cake so that it is tilted away from you. Pipe green lines over the scribed lines to make the daisy chains. Don't pull the piping bag away from the cake as much as required with royal icing as the line will break. Stay fairly close to the cake without touching it.

12 Use the let-down green sugarpaste to stick the daisies to the cake where two loops join.

13 Mix 40g (1½oz) white sugarpaste with ½tsp cooled, boiled water and remove any lumps as before. Fit a piping bag with a no. 6 nozzle and fill it with white sugarpaste. Pipe shells around the bottom edge of the cake.

14 Attach a length of yellow ribbon around the cake drum to finish.

Doll's House and Patchwork Cake

Vegan pastillage takes a little longer to dry than regular pastillage. You will need to make the doll's house in advance and allow three or four days of extra drying time for large or thick pieces. Leave cut-out pieces of pastillage on a wooden chopping board or piece of cardboard to dry: this helps the underneath to dry and will prevent warping.

Edibles

20cm (8") round cake covered in white sugarpaste, secured on a thin cake board the same size

Vegan and gluten-free pastillage: white, see page 94

Sugarpaste: white

Paste food colour: pink

Dust food colours: pastel pink, rose

Rose water

Equipment

Basic equipment, see pages 26 to 27

28cm (11") round cake drum/board

Patterned cutter for roof (FMM Straight Frill Set 2)

Square cutter set

Large and small blossom cutter set (PME)

Patchwork squares embosser (Patchwork Cutters)

15mm (⁵/₈") width ribbon: pink

Doll's House

1 Copy the house template on page 164 onto baking parchment and cut out.

2 Colour ²/₃ of the pastillage light pink with pink paste colour and roll out.

3 Cut out the door and windows first and then the outside of the front panels to prevent stretching. Cut out the back panel and two side panels from the same paste. I use a long straight-edged cutter to give the panels a neat edge.

4 Roll out a small amount of white pastillage, cut out a door and stick in place. Mark the pattern on the door with a craft knife. ▶

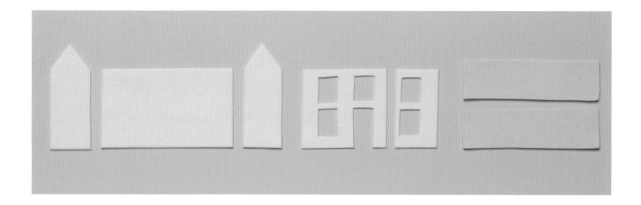

5 To prevent dragging the pastillage out of shape, cut from one edge towards the centre then from the other edge towards the centre.

6 Add a little more pink colouring to the remaining pastillage. Roll out then cut out the roof pieces. Leave on a wooden chopping board or a piece of card to dry. When the pieces have dried they can be assembled with 20g (¾oz) white sugarpaste let-down with ¼tsp cooled, boiled water.

7 Stick the house pieces together and leave to dry before securing the roof in place.

8 Finely roll out some white flower paste. Cut out the window shutters, roof trim and corner pieces and stick to the house using edible glue. Make a chimney and secure this onto the roof with edible glue.

9 Colour a small amount of flower paste with pink paste colour. Roll out finely and cut out several tiny blossoms. Stick these around the door of the house with edible glue.

Cake

10 Press the patchwork squares embosser into the sides of the cake. First emboss the grid, then the patterned squares.

11 Cover the cake drum with white sugarpaste and stick the cake to the cake drum with melted sugarpaste.

12 Place the cake on a turntable and paint the patchwork squares with different shades of pink dust colours diluted with vodka or rose water.

13 Mix 20g (¾oz) pink sugarpaste with ¼tsp cooled, boiled water and fill a piping bag fitted with a no. 1 nozzle.

14 Finely roll out some white flower paste. Cut out lots of large blossoms and slightly soften the edges with a ball tool. Push the ball tool softly into the centre of each blossom to shape.

15 Stick the blossoms around the top and bottom edge of the cake with the let-down sugarpaste. Pipe pink centres in the blossoms.

16 Stick the doll's house on top with the sugarpaste and attach a length of pink ribbon around the cake board to finish.

Peony Wedding Cake

This cake uses sugarpaste shapes for decoration and brush embroidery using watered-down sugarpaste. The peony is made using the vegan flower paste recipe on page 93 and is best made in advance so that it can simply be placed on top of the cake before serving.

Edibles

15cm, 23cm and 30cm (6", 9" and 12") round cakes on cake boards the same size

Sugarpaste: 3kg (6lb 10oz) sage green, 1.5kg (2lb 3oz) white

Flower paste: white

Modelling paste (half flower paste and half sugarpaste): white

Paste food colour: Holly/Ivy (dark green)

Dust food colours: Daffodil (yellow), Holly/Ivy (dark green), Rose (pink), Vine

Edible glue

Rose water

Equipment

Basic equipment, see pages 26 to 27

38cm (15") cake drum/board

Floral wires: 20- and 26-gauge

Tealight

Set of three peony or rose petal cutters: 60mm, 50mm, 45mm (2¼", 2", 1¾") (Tinkertech Two) (or use real petals to make templates)

Tree peony leaf cutters (Tinkertech Two) (or use real petals to make templates)

Rose petal cutter: 35mm (1⅜") (Tinkertech Two)

Tree peony leaf and petal veiners (SK-GI)

Peony template (see page 164)

Floral tape: light green

Hammerhead stamens: white or yellow

Piping nozzles: nos. 1, 1.5

Small block of clear acrylic

Multi ribbon cutter (FMM)

2cm (¾") circle cutter

15mm (⅝") width ribbon: white

Buds

1 Cut a 20-gauge wire in two and bend a small hook at one end of each. Roll two balls of flower paste to about the size of a cherry. Heat the hooked end of each wire over the flame of a tealight and push into each ball of paste. This will ensure the wire sticks securely as the balls of flower paste are quite heavy.

2 Roll out some white flower paste finely. Cut out six 45mm (1¾") peony or rose petals. Emboss the petals in the veiner and frill the edges of three of them.

3 Brush one un-frilled petal with rose water and attach to a bud. Brush the other two un-frilled petals and stick them over the top so they overlap slightly.

4 Moisten the other three petals with rose water and stick around the other bud so they overlap each other slightly. Scrunch the ends together to hide the ball of paste underneath. Brush with Rose dust colour, starting at the base and brushing upwards. Hold the buds in the steam of a kettle for a few seconds to set the colour.

5 Finely roll out a small amount of white flower paste and cut out six 35mm (1³⁄₈") rose petals. Slightly frill the edge with a cocktail stick. Dust with a mixture of Holly/Ivy and Vine dust colours and stick three to the base of each bud as calyces.

Peony

6 For the pistil, cut a 26-gauge wire into three and hook the ends. Roll a large pea-sized amount of flower paste onto each wire. Roll into a cone with a sharp point at the top. Tape the wires together so the cones are tight together and bend the three points outwards. Dust with a mixture of Holly/Ivy and Vine dust colours.

7 Take half a bunch of hammerhead stamens and tape around the pistil. Dilute a little Daffodil dust colour with vodka or rose water and brush over the stamens.

8 Cut each of the seven 26-gauge wires into three. Roll a very thin sausage of flower paste the length of a petal onto each wire. Place under a Flexi-Mat to prevent them from drying out.

9 Roll out the white flower paste finely. Cut out nine tree peony petals or 50mm (2") rose petals and twelve 60mm (2¼") petals. Push the flower paste out of the cutter using a small paintbrush. Place under the Flexi-Mat.

10 One at a time, place the smaller petals on the veiner with the front facing down. Place a wire with the thin sausage of flower paste centrally on top and push down with the other side of the veiner. This will attach the wire to the petal whilst veining the petal. Frill the edge with a cocktail stick.

11 Dust the petals with Rose dust colour, starting at the bottom of the petal and brushing upwards about ¾ of the way up.

12 Tape three petals around the stamens and cup the petals by bending the wire to shape. Cup the remaining six petals the same way and tape around the first three.

13 Vein and frill the 12 larger petals in the same way. Dust with Rose dust colour and cup the petals.

14 Tape six petals around the smaller petals, then tape the final six petals around the outside and play around with them until you are happy with the shape. Roll out a small amount of white flower paste finely and cut out five 35mm (1³⁄₈") rose petals. Slightly frill the edges with a cocktail stick. Dust with a mixture of Holly/Ivy and Vine dust colours and stick to the back of the open peony as a calyx.

15 Pass the flower through the steam of a kettle to set the colours. Hang the flower upside down while you make the leaves.

Leaves

16 If you do not have a tree peony leaf cutter, trace around real peony leaves of slightly different sizes onto a piece of baking parchment and cut out the shapes.

17 Cut five 26-gauge wires in half. Roll a thin sausage of flower paste the same length as the leaf onto nine wires. Place under a Flexi-Mat to prevent them from drying out.

TOP TIP Assemble the flower and leaves while the paste is still soft enough to bend the petals into shape to prevent breakages.

18 Roll out a small amount of white flower paste finely. Cut out three larger leaves and six smaller leaves (three of the left-facing and three of the right-facing leaves). Place a leaf onto the leaf veiner with a wire on top and press in the veiner. Repeat with the rest of the leaves.

19 Dust with a mixture of Holly/Ivy and Vine dust colours and pass through the steam of a kettle quickly to set the colours. Bend into shape.

Flower assembly

20 Tape one of each leaf together from just underneath the leaves. Leave the largest leaf in the centre and attach the two smaller leaves either side of this.

21 Wind green floral tape around the wire of each bud. Tape the buds together from 2.5cm (1") down the wires. Tape one set of leaves underneath the buds.

22 Tape one set of leaves just below the open peony. Continue taping down the stem and add the other set of leaves about 1cm (³/8") further down.

Tape down the stem another 2.5cm (1") then tape the buds in place. Arrange the flower as pictured on page 151 and keep in a safe place until you are ready to make the cake.

Finishing the cake

23 Colour 3kg (6lb 10oz) sugarpaste with dark green paste colour to make a sage green and cover the 15cm and 30cm (6" and 12") cakes and the 38cm (15") cake drum. Place the 15cm (6") cake board centrally on top of the 30cm (12") cake and lightly mark around it with a sharp knife or scribing needle.

24 Trace the peony design on page 164 onto a piece of parchment paper. Turn the paper over and draw over the template again so it is now back-to-front.

25 Place 20g (³/4oz) white sugarpaste onto a plate and add ¼tsp cooled, boiled water. Paddle the sugarpaste on a plate with a small, cranked palette knife to remove any lumps. Put into a paper piping bag fitted with a no. 1 nozzle. Place the piece of acrylic on top

of the back-to-front peony and pipe the peony design onto the acrylic. Leave to dry.

26 Stick the 30cm (12") cake onto the cake drum. On a work surface dusted with a little icing sugar, thinly roll out the white modelling paste. Use the multi-ribbon cutter to cut out 13 strips measuring 2cm (³/4") wide, another 13 measuring 1cm (⁵/8") wide and 13 measuring 5mm (¼") wide. Cover the strips with a Flexi-Mat to stop them drying out.

27 Brush the back of one 2cm (³/4") strip with edible glue and place down the side of the cake. Paste from just above the line marked on top of the cake to the bottom edge. Place another 2cm (³/4") strip directly opposite the first strip down the other side of the cake.

28 Place 2cm (³/4") strips at equal distances down each side of the cake. When they are in the right place, stick them to the cake with edible glue. In between these strips, place the 1cm (³/8") and 5mm (¼") wide strips close together but still leaving a slight gap

as in the picture. When they are in the right place, stick them to the cake with edible glue.

29 Insert dowels into this cake using the dowelling guide on page 163.

30 Knead the white sugarpaste and use to cover the 23cm (9") cake. Use the piped peony on acrylic to emboss the sugarpaste by pressing it gently into the icing and lift off. Emboss all over the cake. If you don't have a piece of clear acrylic, you can scribe the design onto the cake.

31 Place the cake on a turntable so you are ready to brush embroider it.

32 Mix 20g (¾oz) white sugarpaste with ¼tsp cooled, boiled water. Remove any lumps as before, fit a piping bag with a no. 1 nozzle and fill with the sugarpaste.

33 Colour 10g (½oz) sugarpaste with Rose paste colour and mix with ⅛tsp cooled, boiled water. Fit a piping bag with a no. 1 nozzle then fill the bag with the sugarpaste.

34 Mix 20g (¾oz) green sugarpaste with ¼tsp cooled, boiled water, fit a piping bag with a no. 1 nozzle and fill with the sugarpaste. Have a cup of pre-boiled water and a paintbrush ready.

35 Colour 10g (½oz) sugarpaste with Daffodil food paste colour. Mix with ⅛tsp cooled, boiled water and use to fill a piping bag fitted with a no. 1 nozzle.

36 Starting with the petal furthest away from the centre of the design, pipe around the outline with the white icing. Pipe a small line of pink just below this. Dip the paintbrush in the water and blot on a kitchen towel. Place the damp brush on the white piped line, pull the paintbrush down the petal and pull through the pink colour. Clean the brush in the water and blot on kitchen roll. Put the brush on the white line again next to the last stroke and repeat over the whole petal.

37 Repeat with the next petal in, and continue until all petals are coloured. Pipe around the outline with white icing.

38 Use the green let-down paste to repeat the process with the leaves.

39 Pipe on the stamens with yellow icing and leave to dry.

40 Insert dowels into the 23cm (9") cake using the guide.

41 Place a small ball of sugarpaste into a dish with a little water. Heat in the microwave for a few seconds, stir and pour on top of the 30cm (12") cake.

42 Sit the 23cm (9") cake on top then stick the 15cm (6") cake on top of this.

43 Finely roll out white flower paste. Cut out 2cm (¾") circles and stick randomly to the 15cm (6") cake with edible glue.

44 Attach a white ribbon around the base of each cake and the cake drum then secure the peony on top with the let-down white sugarpaste.

SUGARCRAFT PRODUCTS AND THEIR ALLERGENS

Ingredients can change in a product from batch to batch, so always check the label before using for a special diet.

Sugarpaste (rolled fondant)

Manufacturer/Name	Vegan / Vegetarian	Gluten Free?	Dairy Free?	Egg Free?	Nut Free?	Other Information
Renshaw Professional Ready to Roll Icing	Vegan	Gluten free	Dairy free	Egg free	Made in a factory that handles nuts	Glucose derived from wheat but does not contain gluten
Dr Oetker Regal-Ice	Vegan	Gluten free	Dairy free	Egg free	Nut free	Glucose derived from wheat but does not contain gluten
Pettinice	Vegetarian	Made in a factory that handles gluten	Contains dairy	Made in a factory that handles egg	Nut free	Glucose derived from wheat but does not contain gluten
Covapaste	Vegan	Gluten free	Dairy free	Egg free	Nut free	Glucose derived from wheat but does not contain gluten
Silver Spoon Ready to Roll Icing	Vegan	Gluten free	Dairy free	May contain traces of egg	May contain traces of nuts	Glucose derived from wheat but does not contain gluten
M & B Sugarpaste	Vegan	Gluten free	Dairy free	Egg free	Nut free	Glucose derived from wheat but does not contain gluten
Satinice	Vegan	Gluten free	Dairy free	Contains egg	Nut free	
Squires Kitchen Sugarpaste	Vegetarian	Gluten free	Dairy free	May contain traces of egg	May contain traces of nuts	

Marzipan (almond paste)

Manufacturer/Name	Vegan / Vegetarian	Gluten Free?	Dairy Free?	Egg Free?	Nut Free?	Other Information
Squires Kitchen	Vegan	Gluten free	Dairy free	Egg free	Contains nuts	Glucose derived from wheat but does not contain gluten
Odense	Vegan	Contains gluten	Dairy free	Egg free	Contains nuts	Glucose derived from wheat
Ingram Brothers	Vegetarian	Contains gluten	Contains dairy	Egg free	Contains nuts	Glucose derived from wheat
Dr Oetker	Vegan	Gluten free	Dairy free	Egg free	Contains nuts	Glucose derived from wheat but does not contain gluten
Silver Spoon	Vegan	Gluten free	Dairy free	Egg free	Contains nuts	Glucose derived from wheat but does not contain gluten

Marzipan (almond paste) cont.

Manufacturer/Name	Vegan / Vegetarian	Gluten Free?	Dairy Free?	Egg Free?	Nut Free?	Other Information
Sainsbury's	Vegan	Gluten free	Dairy free	Egg free	Contains nuts	Glucose derived from wheat but does not contain gluten
Waitrose	Vegan	Gluten free	Dairy free	Egg free	Contains nuts	Glucose derived from wheat but does not contain gluten
Asda	Vegan	Gluten free	Dairy free	Egg free	Contains nuts	Glucose derived from wheat but does not contain gluten
Tesco	Vegan	Gluten free	Dairy free	Egg free	Contains nuts	Glucose derived from wheat but does not contain gluten

Flower paste (gum paste)

Manufacturer/Name	Vegan / Vegetarian	Gluten Free?	Dairy Free?	Egg Free?	Nut Free?	Other Information
Squires Kitchen Sugar Florist Paste (SFP)	Vegetarian	Gluten free	Dairy free	Contains egg	May contain traces of nuts	Glucose derived from wheat but does not contain gluten
Sugar City Platinum Paste	Vegan	Gluten free	Dairy free	Egg free	Nut free	
Sugar City Diamond Paste	Vegan	Gluten free	Dairy free	Egg free	Nut free	

Mexican paste (modelling paste)

Manufacturer/Name	Vegan / Vegetarian	Gluten Free?	Dairy Free?	Egg Free?	Nut Free?	Other Information
Squires Kitchen Mexican Modelling Paste (MMP)	Vegetarian	Gluten free	Dairy free	May contain traces of egg	May contain traces of nuts	Glucose derived from wheat but does not contain gluten
Squires Kitchen Instant Mix Mexican Paste	Vegan	Gluten free	Dairy free	Does not contain any egg-containing ingredients	May contain traces of nuts	Glucose derived from wheat but does not contain gluten
Squires Kitchen Sugar Dough	Vegetarian	Gluten free	Dairy free	Does not contain any egg-containing ingredients	May contain traces of nuts	Glucose derived from wheat but does not contain gluten
Squires Kitchen Pastillage	Vegetarian	Gluten free	Dairy free	Contains egg	May contain traces of nuts	
Sugar City Mexican Paste	Vegan	Gluten free	Dairy free	Egg free	Nut free	
Sugar City Modelling Paste	Vegan	Gluten free	Dairy free	Egg free	Nut free	

Fondant icing (poured fondant)

Manufacturer/Name	Vegan / Vegetarian	Gluten Free?	Dairy Free?	Egg Free?	Nut Free?	Other Information
Squires Kitchen Fondant Icing Mix	Vegan	Gluten free	Dairy free	Egg free	May contain traces of nuts	
Tate & Lyle Fondant Icing Sugar	Vegan	Gluten free	Dairy free	Egg free	Nut free	
Silver Spoon Fondant Icing Sugar	Vegan	Gluten free	Dairy free	May contain traces of egg	Nut free	

Chocolate paste (chocolate plastique, modelling chocolate)

Manufacturer/Name	Vegan / Vegetarian	Gluten Free?	Dairy Free?	Egg Free?	Nut Free?	Other Information
Squires Kitchen Dark Modelling Cocoform	Vegetarian	Gluten free	May contain traces of milk	Does not contain any egg-containing ingredients	May contain traces of nuts	Contains soya; glucose derived from wheat but does not contain gluten
Squires Kitchen Milk Modelling Cocoform	Vegetarian	Gluten free	Contains milk	Does not contain any egg-containing ingredients	May contain traces of nuts	Contains soya; glucose derived from wheat but does not contain gluten
Squires Kitchen Modelling Cocoform: Green, Red and White	Vegetarian	Gluten free	Contains milk	Does not contain any egg-containing ingredients	May contain traces of nuts	Contains soya; glucose derived from wheat but does not contain gluten
Squires Kitchen Flavoured Cocoform: Brazillian Orange, Cappuccino, English Mint and Strawberry	Vegetarian except Strawberry	Gluten free	Contains milk	Does not contain any egg-containing ingredients	May contain traces of nuts	Contains soya; glucose derived from wheat but does not contain gluten
Renshaw Luxury Belgian Chocolate Paste	Vegetarian	Gluten free	Contains milk	Egg free	May contain traces of nuts	Glucose derived from wheat but does not contain gluten
Renshaw Luxury White Chocolate Paste	Vegetarian	Gluten free	Contains milk	Egg free	May contain traces of nuts	Glucose derived from wheat but does not contain gluten
Tracey's Cakes Dark Chocolate Covering Paste	Vegetarian	Gluten free	May contain traces of milk	Egg free	May contain traces of nuts	Glucose derived from wheat but does not contain gluten

Dried egg white (albumen)

Manufacturer/Name	Vegan / Vegetarian	Gluten Free?	Dairy Free?	Egg Free?	Nut Free?	Other Information
Squires Kitchen Pure Albumen	Vegetarian	Gluten free	Dairy free	Contains egg	May contain traces of nuts	
Dr Oetker Egg White Powder	Vegetarian	Gluten free	Dairy free	Contains egg	Nut free	
Meri-White	Vegetarian	Contains gluten from wheat	Made in a factory that handles dairy	Contains egg	Made in a factory that handles nuts	Contains wheat

Royal icing mixes

Manufacturer/Name	Vegan / Vegetarian	Gluten Free?	Dairy Free?	Egg Free?	Nut Free?	Other Information
Squires Kitchen Instant Mix Royal Icing	Vegetarian	Gluten free	Dairy free	Contains egg	May contain traces of nuts	
Tate & Lyle Royal Icing Sugar	Vegetarian	Gluten free	Dairy free	Contains egg	Nut free	

Most supermarkets now stock Dr Oetker Writing Icing, which does not contain any of the above allergens (gluten, dairy, egg or nuts) and is handy for piping a simple message or decoration. Always check the label as ingredients can change. Alternatively, use watered-down sugarpaste (rolled fondant), which works well piped from a piping nozzle. Water down with pre-boiled water to prevent bacterial growth.

Food colours

Manufacturer/Name	Vegan / Vegetarian	Gluten Free?	Dairy Free?	Egg Free?	Nut Free?	Other Information
Squires Kitchen Dust Food Colours	Vegan	Gluten free	Dairy free	Egg free	May contain traces of nuts	
Squires Kitchen Paste Food Colours	Vegan	Gluten free	Dairy free	Egg free	May contain traces of nuts	Glucose derived from wheat but does not contain gluten
Sugarflair Dust Colours	Vegan	Gluten free	Dairy free	Egg free	Nut free	
Sugarflair Paste Colours	Vegan	Gluten free	Dairy free	Egg free	Nut free	
Sugarflair Liquid Colours	Vegan	Gluten free	Dairy free	Egg free	Nut free	

Glucose syrup

Manufacturer/Name	Vegan / Vegetarian	Gluten Free?	Dairy Free?	Egg Free?	Nut Free?	Other Information
Squires Kitchen Liquid Glucose	Vegetarian	Gluten free	Dairy free	Does not contain any egg-containing ingredients	May contain traces of nuts	Glucose derived from wheat but does not contain gluten
Dr Oetker Liquid Glucose	Vegan	Gluten free	Dairy free	Egg free	Nut free	Glucose derived from wheat but does not contain gluten
Silver Spoon Liquid Glucose	Vegan	Gluten free	Dairy free	Egg free	Nut free	Glucose derived from wheat but does not contain gluten

Allergy advice for Squires Kitchen products

Manufacturer/Name	Vegan / Vegetarian	Gluten Free?	Dairy Free?	Egg Free?	Nut Free?	Other Information
SK Professional Paste Food Colours	Vegan	Gluten free	Dairy free	Egg free	May contain traces of nuts	Glucose derived from wheat but does not contain gluten
SK Professional Dust Food Colours and Lustre Dust Food Colours	Vegan	Gluten free	Dairy free	Egg free	May contain traces of nuts	
SK Professional Liquid Food Colours	Vegan	Gluten free	Dairy free	Egg free	May contain traces of nuts	
SK Professional Food Colour Pens	Vegan	Gluten free	Dairy free	Egg free	May contain traces of nuts	
SK Edible Gold and Silver Effect Paint	Not suitable for vegetarians or vegans	Gluten free	Dairy free	Egg free	May contain traces of nuts	
SK Scintillo Piping Sparkles	Vegan	Gluten free	Dairy free	Egg free	May contain traces of nuts	Glucose derived from wheat but does not contain gluten
SK Dark Modelling Cocoform	Vegetarian	Gluten free	May contain milk	Does not contain any egg-containing ingredients	May contain traces of nuts	Contains soya; glucose derived from wheat but does not contain gluten
SK Milk Modelling Cocoform	Vegetarian	Gluten free	Contains milk	Does not contain any egg-containing ingredients	May contain traces of nuts	Contains soya; glucose derived from wheat but does not contain gluten
SK Modelling Cocoform: Cappuccino, Green, Red and White	Vegetarian	Gluten free	Contains milk	Does not contain any egg-containing ingredients	May contain traces of nuts	Contains soya; glucose derived from wheat but does not contain gluten
SK Strawberry Modelling Cocoform	Not suitable for vegetarians or vegans	Gluten free	Contains milk and soya	Does not contain any egg-containing ingredients	May contain traces of nuts	Glucose derived from wheat but does not contain gluten
SK Dark Belgian Chocolate Couverture	Vegetarian	Gluten free	Contains milk	Does not contain any egg-containing ingredients	May contain traces of nuts	Contains soya
SK Milk Belgian Chocolate Couverture	Vegetarian	Gluten free	Contains milk	Does not contain any egg-containing ingredients	May contain traces of nuts	Contains soya

Allergy advice for Squires Kitchen products cont.

Manufacturer/Name	Vegan / Vegetarian	Gluten Free?	Dairy Free?	Egg Free?	Nut Free?	Other Information
SK Belgian White Chocolate	Vegetarian	Gluten free	Contains milk	Egg free	May contain traces of nuts	Contains soya
SK Cocoa Butter	Vegetarian	Gluten free	May contain traces of milk	Egg free	May contain traces of nuts	
SK CoKrystal B Powdered Cocoa Butter	Vegan	Gluten free	Dairy free	Egg free	May contain traces of nuts	
SK Extra Brute Cocoa Powder	Vegan	Gluten free	May contain milk	Egg free	May contain traces of nuts	
SK Cocol Colourings for Chocolate	Vegetarian	Gluten free	May contain traces of milk	Does not contain any egg-containing ingredients	May contain traces of nuts	
SK Sugar Florist Paste (SFP)	Vegetarian	Gluten free	Dairy free	Contains egg	May contain traces of nuts	Glucose derived from wheat but does not contain gluten
SK Mexican Modelling Paste (MMP)	Vegetarian	Gluten free	Dairy free	May contain traces of egg	May contain traces of nuts	Glucose derived from wheat but does not contain gluten
SK Instant Mix Mexican Paste	Vegetarian	Gluten free	Dairy free	Contains egg	May contain traces of nuts	Glucose derived from wheat but does not contain gluten
SK Sugar Dough	Vegetarian	Gluten free	Dairy free	May contain traces of egg	May contain traces of nuts	Glucose derived from wheat but does not contain gluten
SK CMC Gum	Vegan	Naturally gluten free	Dairy free	Does not contain any egg-containing ingredients	May contain traces of nuts	
SK Gum Tragacanth	Vegan	Naturally gluten free	Dairy free	Does not contain any egg-containing ingredients	May contain traces of nuts	
SK Gum Arabic	Vegan	Naturally gluten free	Dairy free	Does not contain any egg-containing ingredients	May contain traces of nuts	
SK Glucose Syrup	Vegetarian	Gluten free	Dairy free	Does not contain any egg-containing ingredients	May contain traces of nuts	Glucose derived from wheat but does not contain gluten
SK Edible Glue	Vegan	Gluten free	Dairy free	Egg free	May contain traces of nuts	
SK Glycerine	Vegan	Gluten free	Dairy free	Egg free	May contain traces of nuts	
SK Piping Gel	Vegan	Gluten free	Dairy free	Does not contain any egg-containing ingredients	May contain traces of nuts	Glucose derived from wheat but does not contain gluten. Contains sulphur dioxide
SK Leaf Gelatine	Not suitable for vegetarians or vegans	Naturally gluten free	Dairy free	Does not contain any egg-containing ingredients	May contain traces of nuts	
SK Confectioners' Glaze	Not suitable for vegetarians or vegans	Naturally gluten free	Dairy free	Does not contain any egg-containing ingredients	May contain traces of nuts	
SK Fruit Fondant Icing Mix	Vegan	Naturally gluten free	Dairy free	Does not contain any egg-containing ingredients	May contain traces of nuts	Maltodextrin derived from wheat

Allergy advice for Squires Kitchen products cont.

Manufacturer/Name	Vegan / Vegetarian	Gluten Free?	Dairy Free?	Egg Free?	Nut Free?	Other Information
SK Real Fruit Powders	Vegan	Naturally gluten free	Dairy free	Does not contain any egg-containing ingredients	May contain traces of nuts	
SK Instant Mix Bridal Icing Sugar	Vegetarian	Naturally gluten free	Dairy free	Egg free	May contain traces of nuts	
SK Marzipan	Vegan	Gluten free	Dairy free	Egg free	Contains nuts	Glucose derived from wheat but does not contain gluten
SK Hazelnut & Orange Nut Paste	Vegan	Gluten free	Dairy free	Does not contain any egg-containing ingredients	Contains nuts	Glucose derived from wheat but does not contain gluten
SK Almond & Apricot Instant Mix Marzipan	Vegan	Gluten free	Dairy free	Does not contain any egg-containing ingredients	Contains nuts	Glucose derived from wheat but does not contain gluten
SK Apple & Cinnamon Instant Mix Marzipan	Vegetarian	Gluten free	Contains dairy	Does not contain any egg-containing ingredients	Contains nuts	Glucose derived from wheat but does not contain gluten
SK Instant Mix Chocolate Marzipan	Vegetarian	Gluten free	May contain traces of milk	Does not contain any egg-containing ingredients	Contains nuts	Glucose derived from wheat but does not contain gluten
SK Instant Macaroon Mix	Vegetarian	Gluten free	Contains milk	Contains egg	Contains nuts	
SK Pure Albumen	Vegetarian	Gluten free	Dairy free	Contains egg	May contain traces of nuts	
SK Instant Mix Royal Icing	Vegetarian	Gluten free	Dairy free	Contains egg	May contain traces of nuts	
SK Extension Icing	Vegetarian	Gluten free	Dairy free	Contains egg	May contain traces of nuts	
SK Sugarpaste	Vegetarian	Gluten free	Dairy free	May contain traces of egg	May contain traces of nuts	

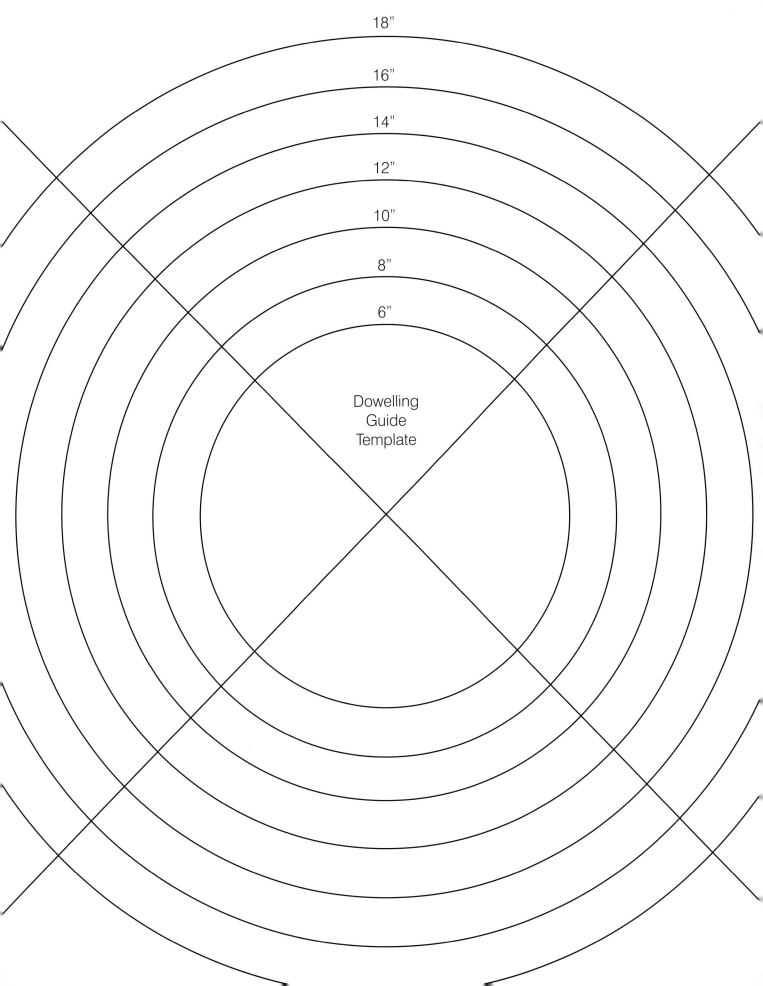

18"
16"
14"
12"
10"
8"
6"

Dowelling
Guide
Template

TEMPLATES

Peony Wedding Cake
Pages 150 to 155

Doll's House and
Patchwork Cake
Pages 147 to 149

GLOSSARY

Almond, soya and coconut milk: Almond milk or soya milk sweetened with apple juice is a great lactose-free alternative to cow's milk. Almond milk tastes just like an almond-flavoured dairy milk whilst sweetened soya milk is as sweet as dairy milk. Coconut milk brings a whole new flavour to a dish!

Allergen: A substance that can cause an allergic reaction.

Allergy: A food allergy is caused when the immune system thinks certain foods are harmful to the body.

Baking parchment: This is a non-stick, strong paper used to line cake tins which prevents cakes sticking to the tin and gives a little protection from the heat.

Cake board: A board used to sit a cake on. A thin board is used when movement is not an issue but if icing a cake, a heavy-duty, hardboard cake board or cake drum should be used.

Cake drum: A cake board about 1cm (½") thick. Used to place underneath a cake to give it firm support and used as a base board under decorated cakes.

Chocolate modelling paste: Made from couverture chocolate and glucose syrup, this can be moulded to make decorations or used to cover a cake.

Coeliac disease: An autoimmune disease. Gluten – which is found in wheat, rye and barley – triggers an immune reaction in people with coeliac disease.

Creaming: Combining sugar and fat.

Cross-contamination (special diets): When a food not containing an allergen is tainted by a food which does contain one.

Dowelling cakes: If something heavy is to be placed on top of a cake such as upper cake tiers, plastic dowels should be placed in the cake to take the weight. I recommend hollow rather than solid dowels for special-diet cakes.

Dummy cake: Polystyrene which is shaped into any cake shape. It can be iced and decorated if a cake is only needed for display, particularly if it needs to be kept for a long time.

Dust food colour: Good for brushing onto the surface of models and flowers for a delicate colour. It can be diluted for painting. It is can also be added to modelling paste and sugarpaste if an intense colour is needed.

Flavourings: Ingredients or chemicals which are used to give a food a stronger flavour.

Flower paste: A modelling paste made from icing sugar, gums and glucose syrup. It can be rolled very fine which is perfect for making sugar flowers and delicate models. It sets very hard.

Folding: Mixing carefully and gently to keep air in a mixture.

Food colours: Available in liquid, paste and dust/powder form.

Glucose syrup: Glucose can be made from any kind of starch and is used in sugary foods to soften texture and prevent the crystallisation of sugars.

Gluten free: A diet or product excluding foods containing gluten such as wheat, barley, rye and oats.

Gluten-free baking powder: A raising agent used in baking. Most brands use wheat flour as a binder but you can buy gluten-free versions which work in exactly the same way. I only use gluten-free baking powder, even for regular baking, so that I never get mixed up.

Glycerine: A food binder which also keeps food moist.

Gum tragacanth: A natural gum which is derived from a plant extract. It helps to allow modelling paste to be rolled out finely and dry firm enough to hold its shape.

Lactose or dairy free: A diet or food excluding all dairy products, i.e. products made from the milk of any animal.

Liquid food colour: This is most often used for colouring royal icing and buttercream.

Maize flour: Known as corn flour in America, this is yellow and milled as fine as flour.

Marzipan: A pliable paste made from ground almonds and glucose syrup. It is used as a cake covering and to make models.

Mexican paste/modelling paste: Not as strong as flower paste but can be used to make models and material-effect cake decorations.

Palette knife: A blunt knife used in baking for spreading, filling and lifting cakes and biscuits.

Paste food colour: Most often used for colouring modelling paste.

Pastillage: A paste made using icing sugar, cornflour, gums and gelatine (or vegetarian alternative) which sets very hard. This means you can cut large panels from it and they will hold their shape, which is good for making plaques and replica buildings. Although it is edible, I would not recommend eating pastillage decorations because it dries so hard.

Rose water: Made from rose petals. It is used in sugarcraft to water down dust colours and to stick light decorations onto cakes or sugar models.

Royal icing: An icing made using egg white and icing sugar which can be spread and piped.

Sifting: To put a fine substance such as flour through a sieve to remove any lumps. It is particularly important to use a sieve when baking gluten-free cakes containing self-raising flour.

Sugarpaste or rolled fondant: A smooth, pliable paste made using icing sugar and glucose syrup. Used as a cake covering and to make models.

Vegan: A person who chooses to avoid eating or using animal products.

Vege-gel: A vegetarian alternative to gelatine.

INDEX

Organisations

Coeliac UK
www.coeliac.co.uk
A charity which provides support and advice for people with coeliac disease and dermatitis herpetiformis (DH).

Food Reactions
www.foodreactions.org
A website giving information about food intolerance and allergy.

Vegan Society
www.vegansociety.com
An organisation which gives information about vegan food and diets, including nutritional advice.

Foods Matter
www.foodsmatter.com
An active website brimming with articles and the very latest research on allergies, intolerance, sensitivity and related health conditions.

Food Standards Agency
www.food.gov.uk
A government website which gives advice and information about food, including legislation and regulations surrounding allergies.

NHS
www.nhs.uk/conditions/food-allergy
Provides a comprehensive body of medical advice about food allergies, their causes, symptoms, diagnosis and treatment.

Iced Gem Bakes
www.icedgembakes.co.uk
My own website which gives lots of advice about baking for special diets and over 130 gluten- and dairy-free recipes.

Trading Standards
www.tradingstandards.gov.uk
A UK government agency that advises and enforces company compliance with trade legislation.

Suppliers

Specialist foods

Doves Farm
www.dovesfarm.co.uk
Doves Farm produce a wide variety of gluten-free and wheat-free products including bread flours, plain and speciality flours, a breakfast cereal and a range of cookies.

Community Foods
www.communityfoods.co.uk
Natural and organic dried food suppliers to retail and wholesale customers.

Plamil Foods
www.plamilfoods.co.uk
Makers of dairy-, nut- and gluten-free chocolate, including very good dairy- and gluten-free chocolate chips and plain chocolate with 60% cocoa solids. No dairy products or nuts are used anywhere in their factory, and products are available to buy in bulk through their website which is great if you use a lot of chocolate.

The Vegan Store
www.theveganstore.com
Online shop selling an amazing range of vegan and gluten-free sweets and chocolate as well as other food staples.

Equipment

Alan Silverwood cake tins
www.alansilverwood.co.uk
Choosing the right cake tin can make a huge difference to your results, and I can highly recommend these tins. They are brilliant for evenly baking a mixture and give cakes a lovely colour. Just as importantly, the coating does not rust or flake and they are very easy to clean, essential when baking special-diet cakes. Found in good cook shops.

If You Care
www.ifyoucare.com
Makers of 100% recycled aluminium foil and unbleached baking parchment. This is a brilliant baking parchment that doesn't need greasing. It is really strong so good for paper piping bags too. It can also be used again if clean and can be composted after use.

Nisbets
www.nisbets.co.uk
Catering equipment suppliers. This is where I buy my nylon piping bags, Savoy nozzles and a good-quality carving knife.

Sugarcraft equipment and specialist cake ingredients

Squires Kitchen
www.squires-shop.com
Over 6,000 cake decorating products including a wide range of food colourings, sugar pastes and icings, bakeware and ready-made decorations. Includes a section on special diets. Worldwide mail order available.

A Piece of Cake
www.sugaricing.com
Cake decorating shop and website.